PRAYERS FROM THE CLOUD

PRAYERS
from the
CLOUD

100 PRAYERS
THROUGH THE AGES

PETE JAMES

WILLIAM B. EERDMANS PUBLISHING COMPANY

GRAND RAPIDS, MICHIGAN

Wm. B. Eerdmans Publishing Co.
4035 Park East Court SE, Grand Rapids, Michigan 49546
www.eerdmans.com

Book design by Lydia Hall

Printed in the United States of America

31 30 29 28 27 26 25   1 2 3 4 5 6 7

ISBN 978-0-8028-8470-1

Library of Congress Cataloging-in-Publication Data

A catalog record for this book is available from the Library of Congress.

We are surrounded by so great a cloud of witnesses . . .

—Hebrews 12:1

We must dedicate this offering with our whole heart.
We must fatten it on faith,
tend it by truth,
keep it unblemished through innocence
and clean through chastity,
and crown it with love.
We must escort it to the altar of God
in a procession of good works
to the sound of psalms and hymns.
Then it will gain for us all that we ask of God.

—Tertullian, *On Prayer*

Contents

Preface: Early to Christ, Late to Pray

I came to Christ at age nineteen, early in my adult life. I came to prayer much later in life. Sure, I prayed as a new believer, but only in fits and starts. Preachers stressed the importance of a regular "quiet time," which was code in the church for having a daily routine of Bible reading and prayer. I tried to have a quiet time but couldn't get past the notion that the exercise seemed, well, too quiet! I wanted action. I wanted to do something for God, build something for God, leap tall buildings in a single bound for God. The thought of simply *being* with God did not interest me enough to incorporate prayer into my daily life.

I joined a campus ministry with my wife, Chris, to reach college students for Christ. I did a credible job introducing them to Jesus, but I couldn't take them very far in the journey. I didn't know beans about the Bible, and I wasn't very good at prayer. I went to seminary to become biblically literate and earn my religious credentials. I was well suited to seminary—pursuing the life of the mind invigorated me. After graduation, I was called to pastor a church in metro DC.

About ten years into ministry, I hit the wall. It wasn't one of those obvious crash-and-burn scenarios that sometimes happen to people in midlife. My burnout was of the subtle variety. I was empty inside, feeling like a fake, extolling the virtues of living the spiritual life without intentionally practicing the disciplines that cultivate them. I knew in my soul I wasn't going to make it in ministry over the long haul in my present circumstances. Something inside me said, "Go deeper." I didn't so much as hear God's voice. Lord knows if God spoke to me in the middle of the night, I might freak out. God's call was a still, quiet whisper, the kind Elijah experienced.

So, I made three changes.

First, I began reading the Bible for things other than sermon preparation. This new practice came easily to me since I like to read. Yet I had to learn how to read slowly and reflectively. Meditative reading isn't like reading beach novels. I discovered in the process of reading the Bible that it was reading me. This became uncomfortable at times. No doubt, it was one reason why I put it off so long. I didn't want the Bible to bring my assorted flaws to the surface.

Second, I started to pray regularly. This was a harder discipline for me to develop. I'm not a contemplative person by nature, or so I reasoned to myself. Let other people do the praying. I'll do the preaching. But it doesn't work this way. There's no way to do God's work apart from being with God. In the words of the Puritan John Flavel, "The greatest difficulty before conversion is to win the heart to God, and the greatest difficulty after conversion is to keep the heart with God."

The Psalms became my tutorial on how to pray. Someone suggested I develop the habit of reading one psalm each day as though I were the person praying it. Whereas I was used to praying mostly about nice things and what I wanted God to do for me, the Psalms, I discovered, pray about everything. They express to God deep gratitude and unbridled joy as well as anguish over betrayal, grief over loss, penitence over sin, and vengeful feelings toward enemies. The Psalms taught me to bring my whole self to God in prayer.

Third, I let people into my life. Chris and I joined a small group of parents our age to pray for our kids. We were weary from stressing about our emerging teens as we sat on metal bleachers at baseball games. Why don't we pray for them? What a novel idea! I also signed on to two small groups of pastoral colleagues. I learned how to get past surface chatter to talk about my real life. God used prayer with other people as one way to reorder my life.

I still longed to build a dynamic church ministry, the kind I had read about in Christian periodicals. Yet a titanic shift was already underway. I was moving, to borrow Eugene Peterson's words, from being a competitive pastor to becoming a contemplative one.

Still, after all these years, prayer doesn't come easily to me. I am still a novice when it comes to prayer. There are days when I rattle off my list of concerns to God in rapid-fire succession. My mind wanders and I stare at the ceiling. Why am I not more effusive and thankful? Why can't I sustain my prayers for more than five minutes? Thomas Merton was a monk whose life was marked by regular, disciplined prayer. I am encouraged by something he wrote: "We do not want to be beginners [at prayer], but let us be convinced that we will never be anything but beginners, all our lives."

I am an avid reader of history. It's the best way I know to escape the characteristic illusions of our modern age. In recent times, I have incorporated the practice of reading old prayers. This started in earnest when I retired and was sorting through old books. I came upon one I had never read, *2000 Years of Prayer*. I opened it and read a few prayers from the first few centuries of the church. I was hooked. Early Christians knew how to pray. I can draft off these prayers, I thought. And so, I did.

I started sending prayers from church history to a cousin in 2022 who had serious back surgery and was quarantined for possible COVID. She texted me from the ICU that she felt all alone. My pastoral proclivities went into high alert. "You're never alone," I reminded her. "God is with you." She was an active churchgoer who knew this message in her bones, but the extremis of her predicament caused her to lose sight of this fundamental reality. Since I had just been reading old prayers, I offered to send some her way. She accepted. I kept the prayers going for a few weeks until she felt better, and I ran out of readily available material. After a time, she wrote to tell me she missed the prayers. "Do you have any more?" she asked.

How could I say no? So I resumed sending her prayers. Then she asked, "Who are all these people? I've never heard of them." I then began adding brief narratives about the people who originated the prayers.

Finding prayers at the beginning wasn't hard since I sent the ones I knew and loved. It wasn't long before I cycled through my favorites, and it became more challenging. I was running out of prayers and had to take a deeper dive. I felt like a miner, digging into the forgotten past, in places I had never been before. I had never heard of many of the people I've uncovered in this prayer dig.

Praying other people's prayers rubs off on me. I'm inspired and humbled by their stories. Their accounts of privation and hardship stir something deep in me. Some of the people in this "great cloud of witnesses" had it bad. Real bad. Remind me never, ever to complain again. I came to realize these prayers were not only for my dear cousin. They were for me. It's me, Lord, standin' in the need of prayer.

It occurred to me that other people might also like these prayers, so I began to send them over an email list to family and close friends. Word got out and others joined in. I recruited an IT assistant and sent out two years' worth of prayers—730, to be exact. So much work. So many blessings.

The disciples asked Jesus to teach them how to pray. We have no record that they ever requested Jesus's help in learning how to preach or lead worship. But they needed Jesus to teach them how to pray. Jesus didn't comply with their request by giving them a lecture on the logistics of prayer. He taught them to pray by praying. That's how the Lord's Prayer came to us. Some people balk at written prayers, preferring instead free-form, spontaneous prayers. But doesn't the Lord's Prayer come to us in written form? The Psalms are scripted as well. That doesn't negate our ability to pray them from the heart. So, too, the prayers of others across time.

What follows in these pages are one hundred prayers from the first year of my Prayers from the Cloud project. For the complete collection of these prayers, you can go to https://prayersfromthecloud.com. After two years of reading and reflecting on other people's prayers, let me give a witness: we learn to pray by praying!

I am grateful that my former church history professor, Garth Rosell, encouraged me to keep writing, despite the obstacles. Cousin Elizabeth Berberich did her part in receiving these prayers and asking for more. Chris Anderson came to my rescue in creating Prayersfromthecloud.com. Early input from Tom Petter, Stan Ott, and Mark Labberton helped considerably, as did the support of son Andrew, daughter Emily, and their families. I am thankful that sister-in-law Debbie James sent the prayers to Hearts & Minds bookstore owner Byron Borger, who thought enough of this project to pass it along to publishers. I appreciate the guidance of Andrew Knapp with Eerdmans and Victoria Jones in her highly capable role as editor. Most of all, I give thanks to my wife, Chris, whose wise counsel was invaluable and whose enthusiasm for these prayers from the past kept me motivated.

PRAYERS
through the AGES

Polycarp

Polycarp (69–155) was the last surviving link to Jesus's original twelve apostles, having been a student of the apostle John. Polycarp served as bishop of Smyrna and was a respected leader in the early church. When the Roman Empire unleashed a new wave of persecutions against Christians, Polycarp was informed that Roman officials were coming to arrest him. While panic-stricken friends urged him to flee, he calmly waited for his captors at his home. When they arrived, Polycarp requested food and drink be served to them. He made only one request: one hour to pray before they took him away.

The officers who overheard him praying began to have second thoughts. Why were they arresting a devout old man like this? He was taken to the proconsul Quadratus, who ordered him to offer incense before a statue of the emperor and deny allegiance to Christ. Polycarp refused, saying, "For eighty and six years I have served him, and he has done me no wrong. How can I blaspheme my King and Savior who has saved me?" When the proconsul urged him to reconsider, Polycarp stood his ground and was subsequently burned at the stake. His candid prayer challenges us to do likewise.

O Lord God Almighty, the Father of your beloved and blessed Son Jesus Christ, by whom we have received the knowledge of you, the God of angels and powers, and of every creature, and of all the righteous who live before you, I give you thanks that you count me worthy to be numbered among your martyrs, sharing the cup of Christ and the resurrection to eternal life, both of soul and body, through the immortality of the Holy Spirit. May I be received this day as an acceptable sacrifice, as you, the true God, have predestined, revealed to me, and now fulfilled. I praise you for all these things, I bless and glorify you, along with the everlasting Jesus Christ, your beloved Son. To you, with him, through the Holy Ghost, be glory now and forever. Amen.

Irenaeus of Lyons

Dating back to the second century, this prayer originated with Irenaeus of Lyons (in modern-day France) (130–202). Irenaeus was introduced to Christ through Polycarp, who was said to have been taught by the apostle John.

We owe Irenaeus a debt of gratitude for resisting a heretical movement called Gnosticism. His most influential work, *Against Heresies*, written in AD 180, sounded the alarm for this early departure from biblical Christianity. Gnostics believed Jesus was divine but not truly human, so he did not really die on the cross to offer his life as an atonement for sins. The implications of this defection were far-reaching, and it would explain why numerous letters in the New Testament have this false teaching in their sights. Irenaeus clearly articulated that Jesus is both fully human and fully divine, a central affirmation of the Christian faith. Keep in mind that the New Testament canon had not yet been resolved. Irenaeus made extensive use of all four Gospels and all but four of the New Testament epistles, thereby demonstrating that many of these writings were already considered authoritative by the church. He observed the subtle way heresies gained a hearing in the church. "Error never shows itself in its naked reality, in order not to be discovered. On the contrary, it dresses elegantly, so that the unwary may be led to believe that it is more truthful than truth itself," he wrote.

Irenaeus was instrumental in guiding the early church in its infancy. His name, meaning "peacemaker," fits him well, since peacemaking was his lasting contribution.

Give maturity to beginners, O Father;
give intelligence to the little ones;
give aid to those who are running their course.
Give sorrow to the negligent;
give fervor of spirit to the lukewarm.
Give to those in their older years a good consummation,
for the sake of Jesus Christ our Lord.
Amen.

Eusebius of Caesarea

Author Owen Barfield used to chide his agnostic literary colleague C. S. Lewis for his "chronological snobbery" in his early years. Barfield coined this phrase to describe the attitude that the present is superior to the past. Doesn't the same attitude hold in our own time? We boast about our technology and increased efficiency. We pat ourselves on the back for our heightened levels of tolerance. Clearly, our arrogance is showing. One reason we read history is to unmask the illusions and distortions of our current age.

Eusebius of Caesarea (ca. 260–340) has been called the father of church history. His detailed review of church history from the time of the apostles until AD 323 is one of a kind. His purpose was to connect the fourth-century church of which he was a part to the authentic witness of the early church in following the risen Jesus. Without his extensive ten-volume work, much of what we know of early church history would be lost.

Eusebius's research was not without its prejudices and limitations. He was biased by his affection for Emperor Constantine and harsh in his condemnation of Jews as responsible for Jesus's death. He admitted in the foreword to his history, "I feel inadequate to do it [church history] justice."

Eusebius took a leading role at the Council of Nicaea in 325, which rejected Arius's teaching that the Son was subordinate to the Father. Eusebius delivered the opening address and voted with the majority to adopt the Nicene Creed. He recognized the damage done by Arius's erroneous teaching, yet he also wanted to draw Arius back into the fold and thus did not support the council's decision to excommunicate him.

Eusebius's prayer that follows here seeks to apply Jesus's teaching on the Golden Rule (Matt. 7:12) to everyday relationships.

May I be no one's enemy.
May I be the friend of that which is eternal and abides.
May I never quarrel with those nearest me,
and if I do, may I be reconciled quickly.
May I love, seek, and attain only that which is good.
May I wish for all people's happiness and envy none.
May I never rejoice in the ill fortune of one who has wronged me.
When I have done or said what is wrong,
may I never wait for the rebuke of others,
but always rebuke myself until I make amends.
May I win no victory that harms either me or my opponent.
May I reconcile friends who are angry with one another.
May I never fail a friend who is in danger.
When visiting those in grief,
may I be able by gentle and healing words to soften pain.
May I respect myself.
May I always keep tame that which rages within me.
May I accustom myself to be gentle,
and never angry with people because of circumstances.
May I never discuss who is wicked and what wicked things they have done,
but know good people and follow in their footsteps.
Amen.

Ephrem the Syrian

In his three-volume, eight-hundred-page work *Center Church*, the late pastor Tim Keller devotes the entirety of his second volume to city ministry. He believed it was a primary biblical strategy for the early church to evangelize cities and appealed to churches in the twenty-first century to invest once more in urban welfare.

Not everybody was big into city ministry in the first few centuries of the church. Fourth-century monks sought refuge in the desert to escape the corrupting influence of city life. But Ephrem the Syrian (ca. 306–373) rejected this growing trend toward ascetic isolation. He formed with other like-minded believers a voluntary order called "Members of the Covenant," an intentional urban community of men and women committed to both celibacy and service to their community. They maintained a set-apart lifestyle while maintaining a vital connection to the wider populace.

Ephrem reportedly had an awful singing voice yet became a prolific hymn writer. Four hundred of his hymns still exist and are still sung in Syrian churches today. His hymns were designed primarily as teaching hymns, rich in theological content and intended to refute principal heresies of his day.

O Lord and Master of my life!
Take from me the spirit of laziness,
faint-heartedness, desire for power, and idle talk.
But give your servant the spirit of chastity,
humility, patience, and love.
Yes, Lord and King!
Grant me to see my own errors,
and not to unjustly or hastily judge my brother,
for you are blessed, now and forever.
Amen.

Athanasius

Athanasius (ca. 296–373) was leading worship one Sunday in Alexandria when soldiers stormed the sanctuary to arrest him. Athanasius took it in stride. Before he was escorted out, he instructed his assistant to read aloud Psalm 136. Each of the twenty-six verses ends with the refrain "God's steadfast love endures forever."

Athanasius was accustomed to conflict. He was banished from Alexandria on five different occasions. Seventeen of the forty-five years he served as bishop of Alexandria were spent in exile. His enemies called him "Black Dwarf." This diminutive, dark-skinned Egyptian accumulated lots of enemies over the years. What was his crime? Would you believe his orthodox view of Jesus? The fourth century was an era of considerable debate over Jesus. We're not talking intramural debates over arcane matters. No less than salvation hung in the balance. Athanasius affirmed Jesus's full humanity and divinity. Only one who was fully human could atone for human sins, and only one who was fully divine had the power to save, he insisted. The opposition, led by Arius, rejected Jesus's divinity and denied the Trinity. Arians believed Jesus was a created being. In Arius's words, "There was a time when Christ was not." Athanasius fought this battle alone at times yet refused to back down. He outlasted four emperors who exiled him. They could have just as easily executed him. The conflict over Jesus's identity and mission lasted Athanasius's entire life. Only in his last few years did his beliefs gain wider acceptance.

Athanasius's writings, which he composed in exile, have shaped the church for nearly two millennia. He is the epitome of courage in conflict. This prayer by Athanasius was offered shortly before his death.

Thou art Jesus, the Son of the Father.

    Yea, Amen.

Thou art he who commandeth the cherubim and seraphim.

    Yea, Amen.

Thou hast existed with the Father in truth always.

    Yea, Amen.

Thou rulest the angels.

    Yea, Amen.

Thou art the power of the heavens.

    Yea, Amen.

Thou art the crown of the martyrs.

    Yea, Amen.

Thou art the deep counsel of the saints.

    Yea, Amen.

Thou art he in whom the deep counsel of the Father is hidden.

    Yea, Amen.

Thou art the mouth of the prophets.

    Yea, Amen.

Thou art the tongue of the angels.

    Yea, Amen.

Thou art Jesus, my life.

    Yea, Amen.

Thou art Jesus, the object of the boast of the world.

    Yea, Amen.

Macrina the Younger

Some people do us a favor by putting us in our place. We need people to tell us the truth. We are not as important as we think we are.

Macrina the Younger (ca. 327–379) served this role in the lives of her two famous brothers, Gregory of Nyssa and Basil of Caesarea, influential leaders in the early church. When Gregory returned from university, he found his boyhood home a far different place than he had known before. Macrina had convinced their mom to free the family's slaves and convert the family estate into a Christian community. Macrina shaped its monastic life around three simple practices: prayer, work, and serving others. During a severe drought, she combed the area to find children abandoned by starving parents and adopted them into the community.

Gregory arrived home puffed up with self-importance, having excelled in his studies. His recent success as a public speaker had gone to his head. Macrina wasted no time in bringing him down to earth. She challenged him to put his talents to work in the church and forgo worldly pursuits. He joined her community, which shaped him in profound ways. When in 376, a synod deposed Gregory from his position as bishop and the emperor exiled him, it was Macrina who snapped her brother out of his whining by reminding him to count his blessings and recognize God's favor. "You are renowned in cities and peoples and nations. Churches summon you as an ally and director, and do you not see the grace of God in it all?" she pressed. "Do you fail to recognize the cause of such great blessings, that it is your parents' prayers that are lifting you up on high, you that have little or no equipment within yourself for such success?" Spoken like a true older sister!

Gregory wrote a biography honoring his sister, including their remarkable dialogue as she lay dying. She challenged him to refrain from mourning like an unbeliever and whispered a parting prayer.

You, O Lord, have freed us from the fear of death. You have made the end of this life the beginning to us of true life. . . . You who broke the flaming sword and restored to paradise the man who was crucified with you and implored your mercies, remember me too in your kingdom. . . . Let not the terrible chasm separate me from your elect. Nor let the Slanderer stand against me in the way; nor let my sin be found before your eyes, if in anything I have sinned in word, deed, or thought, led astray by the weakness of my nature. O you who have power on earth to forgive sins, forgive me, that I may be refreshed and may be found before you, when I put off my body, without defilement on my soul. But may my soul be received into your hands spotless and undefiled, as an offering before you.

Gregory of Nyssa

Slavery was considered standard operating procedure in the ancient world. It was deemed necessary to make the mighty Roman Empire economy go. Gregory of Nyssa (ca. 335–ca. 395) was a rare dissenting voice who railed against slavery in sermons and writings. His argument was rather simple. Since the first chapter of Genesis makes plain that God creates people in his image, they are God's and cannot properly belong to anyone else. Gregory said in a sermon, "If we are in the image of God, then who is his buyer, tell me? Who is his seller? To God alone belongs this power, or rather, not even to God himself, for his gracious gifts, it says, are irrevocable. God would not therefore reduce the human race to slavery, since he himself, when we had been enslaved to sin, spontaneously recalled us to faith. If God did not enslave what is free, who is he that sets his own powers against God's?"

Gregory of Nyssa, along with his brother Basil and another Gregory (of Nazianzus), are called the Cappadocian fathers. (Cappadocia was a region in modern-day Turkey.) These three early church leaders articulated a thorough understanding of the nature of our Trinitarian God. Their theology is not merely academic; it bears upon God's people to obey this triune God in condemning slavery. God not only heals the breach caused by sin but also calls people to account for every sin perpetrated against our fellow creatures.

Kindness flows from you, Lord, pure and continual.

You had cast us off, as was only just, but mercifully you forgave us;

you hated us and you were reconciled to us, you cursed us and you
blessed us;

you banished us from paradise, and you called us back again;

you took from us the fig leaves that had made us so unseemly a garment,
and you put on us a cloak of great value;

you opened the prison-gates and gave the condemned a pardon;

you sprinkled us clean with water and washed away the dirt. . . .

Let us, then, sing that joyful hymn which a voice inspired by the Spirit once
sang in prophecy:

"My soul will rejoice in the Lord,

for he has given me salvation for my garment . . ."

Ambrose of Milan

The church was locked in a conflict with the Arians (who insisted God the Father created Jesus the Son, thereby making Jesus a lesser being) over who would be elected the next bishop of Milan. Ambrose (ca. 339–397), who was Milan's governor at the time, was on hand to keep the peace. A chant went up during the proceedings: "Ambrose, bishop." Long story short: Ambrose went from unbaptized layman to church bishop in eight days.

He took his new calling seriously. He spent several hours in daily prayer and adopted an ascetic lifestyle, giving money and land away to the poor. He was willing to stand up to Roman emperors when they interfered in church matters, saying, "The emperor is in the church, not above the church." His major work, *De Fide* (On Faith), established the Nicene Creed as the official church response to the Arian controversy. He used his diplomatic skills to settle debates over local church customs. He wrote, "When I am in Rome, I fast on Saturdays. When I am in Milan, I do not. Follow the custom in the church where you are." This saying led to Ambrose's legendary proverb, "When in Rome, do as the Romans do."

When Augustine was a teacher of rhetoric and still a skeptic, he went to hear Ambrose preach, more to critique his style than to listen to his content. Augustine wrote later in his *Confessions*, "As I opened my heart to recognize how eloquently he was speaking, it occurred to me how truly he was speaking." Augustine credited Ambrose with turning his heart to Scripture, resulting in his conversion.

Ambrose is eminently quotable. Here's but a sample: "No one heals himself by wounding another." "Our evil inclinations are far more dangerous than our external enemies." "Love is like a shadow. One can catch it only by falling into it."

O Lord, you have mercy upon all,
and hate nothing that you have made.
Remember how frail our nature is,
and that you are our Father and our God.
Don't be angry with us forever,
and stop your tender mercies in displeasure.
For it is not for our just works
that we present our prayers before you,
but for the multitude of your tender mercies.
Take away from us, O Lord, our iniquities,
and mercifully kindle in us the fire of your Holy Spirit.
Take away from us a heart of stone,
and give us a heart of flesh,
a heart to love and adore you,
a heart to delight in, to follow, and to enjoy you.
And we entreat your mercy, O Lord,
that you would look down graciously upon your family,
as it pays its vows to your most holy name.
And that the desire of none may be in vain,
and the petitions of none unfulfilled,
inspire our prayers, that they may be
to your delight to hear and answer.

Augustine of Hippo

Augustine (354–430) was restless. He identified his restlessness at the out-set of his autobiography, the *Confessions*: "Thou hast made us for thyself and restless is our heart until it comes to rest in thee." As Augustine looked back over his life in 397 at age forty-three, he described his restless long-ing to fill the ache in his heart with material and pseudospiritual pursuits. He lived with a series of mistresses, fathering a child with one of them. He acknowledged his persistent battle with sexual impurity, as expressed in his famous quote "Give me chastity, O Lord, but not yet." His stealing and frequent lying disclosed his wayward heart. He dabbled in astrology and became infatuated with Manichean philosophy. He summarized his early life this way: "I became to myself a wasteland."

He was sitting in a garden one day, lamenting his poor choices, when he heard a child's voice directing him, "Take up and read." He retrieved a Bible and opened to the words "Let us behave decently, as in the daytime, not in carousing and drunkenness, not in sexual immorality and debauch-ery, not in dissension and jealousy. Rather, clothe yourselves with the Lord Jesus Christ and do not think about how to gratify the desires of the flesh" (Rom. 13:13–14 NIV). He opened his life to Christ and became, outside the apostle Paul, arguably the greatest theologian the church has ever known. I find myself returning to his earlier quote about restlessness often. Our satisfaction cannot be found in romance, wealth, or learning, but only in the One who formed us.

Augustine's *Confessions* was the first literary work of its kind in the annals of church history. "Confession" has a double meaning in this context, as not only was Augustine transparent about confessing his flaws; he was also desirous to confess God's saving mercy.

Too late have I loved you, O Beauty so ancient yet ever new! Too late have I loved you! Behold, you were within, and I abroad, and there I searched for you; deformed I, plunging amid those fair forms which you had made. You were with me, but I was not with you. Things held me far from you, which, unless they were in you, would not exist at all. You called, and shouted, and burst my deafness. You flashed, shone, and scattered my blindness. You breathed odors, and I drew in breath and panted for you. I tasted, and hunger and thirst. You touched me, and I burned for your peace.

Patrick of Ireland

Patrick (ca. 385–461) may be regarded as a saint in the Catholic church, but the opening line of his autobiography, *Confession*, reveals how he viewed himself: "My name is Patrick. I am a sinner." Born along the coast of England, Patrick (or Patricius, his Latin name) was captured by pirates as a teenager, who sold him to Irish slaveholders. He worked under harsh conditions as a herdsman for six years, yet the time spent in captivity awakened his soul to God. He wrote in his autobiography,

> So I am first of all a simple country person, and the least of all the faithful and utterly despised by many. I was about sixteen years of age and did not know the true God when I was taken into captivity in Ireland with many thousands of people. . . . It was there that the Lord opened up my awareness to my lack of faith. I recognized my failings and turned to the Lord with all my heart, who looked down on my lowliness and had mercy on my youthful ignorance. . . . Hence I cannot be silent about such great blessings and grace that the Lord so kindly bestowed on me in the land of my captivity.

Christ appeared to Patrick in a dream and told him a ship was ready to take him back to England. He trekked two hundred miles to the coast, negotiated his way onto a cargo vessel, and arrived safely home. But then he had a second dream, this time a summons to return to Ireland, the place of his former captivity, to preach the gospel. He followed the call, becoming a missionary and helping establish the church in Ireland.

In Celtic Christianity, a popular type of prayer is known as the *lorica* ("breastplate"), a prayer recited for protection. While the following breastplate prayer is often attributed to Patrick, it likely originated in the eighth century. Yet it expresses Patrick's manner of praying and the Celtic Christian spirituality that bears his influence. The beginning segment is an ideal morning prayer.

This day I call to me:
God's strength to direct me,
God's power to sustain me,
God's wisdom to guide me,
God's vision to light me,
God's ear to my hearing,
God's word to my speaking,
God's hand to uphold me,
God's pathway before me,
God's shield to protect me.

. . . .

Christ beside me, Christ before me;
Christ behind me, Christ within me;
Christ beneath me, Christ above me;
Christ to right of me, Christ to left of me;
Christ in my lying, my sitting, my rising;
Christ in heart of all who know me,
Christ on tongue of all who meet me,
Christ in eye of all who see me,
Christ in ear of all who hear me.

For my shield this day I call
a mighty power:
the Holy Trinity!
Amen.

Benedict of Nursia

The Rule of Saint Benedict leaves no stone unturned. It provides guidelines for monastic living on most everything—sleeping, working, traveling, entertaining guests. He even devotes two chapters to addressing day-to-day concerns about drinking (a half measure of wine each day should suffice) and eating (two kinds of cooked foods plus fruits and veggies is optimal); allowances can be made depending on locale and diet restrictions. "Above all else," he writes, "they should live without grumbling."

This matter of grumbling is of primary importance to Benedict (480–547). While he sets up procedures for lodging legitimate complaints in monastic life, he regards murmuring and whining as toxic to these "schools for the soul." Complaining tears at the fabric of the body of Christ. That's why he hits it hard in his seventy-three-chapter manual on community life. Just as a heart murmur can indicate a deeper heart problem, complaining can warn of a spiritual heart defect.

The Bible has plenty to say on this matter of complaining. God's people repeatedly murmur against Moses in the Sinai wilderness. The New Testament letters call out grumbling on multiple occasions. I can attest to its deleterious effect on church life. Whining and complaining have a corrosive influence on community welfare.

Benedict's Rule of Life has served as the gold standard in monastic living for the past fifteen hundred years for good reason. "Do not be a murmurer," Benedict warns. 'Nuff said.

O gracious and holy Father,
give us wisdom to perceive you,
diligence to seek you,
patience to wait for you,
eyes to behold you,
a heart to meditate on you,
and a life to proclaim you,
through the power of the Spirit of Jesus our Lord.
Amen.

Fursey of Ireland

They wore long dark robes complete with hoods. Their tonsures—a ring of hair encircling their shaved heads—added to the mystique. These Irish monks were distinctive both in appearance and in their fervor to spread the gospel across western Europe in the seventh century. Patrick was undoubtedly the most well known, but Fursey (ca. 567–650) deserves some recognition also.

In his early twenties, Fursey had a near-death experience and received three visions to preach the good news of Jesus. He traveled throughout Ireland attracting huge crowds, as people were drawn to his effective preaching and charismatic manner. Disturbed that people wanted to follow him rather than Christ, he established monasteries as centers of learning to train monks thoroughly in the way of Jesus. His mission journeys spread beyond Ireland to England and France.

Fursey is an Old Irish word for virtue. A fellow monk named Bede, who came after him, described Fursey as "outstanding in virtue." Bede wrote that, "inspired by the example of his goodness and the effectiveness of his teaching, many unbelievers were drawn to Christ, and those who already believe were drawn to greater love and faith in him."

One of Fursey's prayers that survives is called the Lorica of St. Fursey. *Lorica* is the Latin term for protective armor. His prayer expresses in classic Celtic manner an appeal for God's complete protection. Irish monks like Fursey ventured into unknown lands relying on Christ to protect them and show them the way.

May the guiding hands of God be on my shoulders,
may the presence of the Holy Spirit be on my head,
may the sign of Christ be on my forehead,
may the voice of the Holy Spirit be in my ears,
may the smell of the Holy Spirit be in my nose,
may the sight of the company of heaven be in my eyes,
may the speech of the company of heaven be in my mouth,
may the work of the church of God be in my hands,
may the serving of God and neighbor be in my feet,
may God make my heart his home,
and may I belong to God, my Father, completely.

Bede the Venerable

The so-called seven deadly sins appear in final form in the late sixth century. I'm not surprised that lethal sins like pride, greed, and envy make the final cut. But sloth? The original Latin word, *acedia*, implies apathy toward the things of God. The word came to prominence in medieval monasteries. Monastic life centered on disciplined intervals of prayer, worship, study, and manual labor. Monks came to regard acedia as "the noonday devil." When it was too hot to work outside in the middle part of the day, monks would retreat to their rooms for prayer and study. It was the time when monks felt most tempted to weariness and deflation of the soul.

Bede (ca. 672–735) came to live at the Wearmouth-Jarrow monastery in England at the tender age of seven. Before we condemn his family for consigning him to a monastery, keep in mind it was the only means available for poor families to educate their sons and provide them with a balanced diet.

Bede lived virtually his entire life in a monastic setting. He was diligent and hardworking. He not only wrote commentaries on Scripture but also found time to compile a history of England. He also conjectured that the moon affected the tides and that the earth is round. He knew firsthand the perils of acedia and warned readers of its insidious dangers.

Spiritual boredom is a killer sin for us moderns also. This prayer by Bede asks for God's help in our struggle with "the grayness of our apathy."

O Christ, our Morning Star,
splendor of Light Eternal,
shining with the glory of the rainbow,
come and waken us
from the grayness of our apathy,
and renew in us your gift of hope.
Amen.

Alcuin of York

One of the most famous swords in history is on display at the Louvre Museum in Paris. It's called the Sword of Joyeuse and is reported to have belonged to Charlemagne. The irony is not lost on me that *joyeuse* in French means "joyful," not a word I would normally associate with a sword. Charlemagne's weapon was emblematic of his militaristic reign in the eighth century over vast portions of western Europe. He wielded the sword to bring Italy, France, Germany, Austria, and the Low Countries into his ever-expanding empire. He sought to make Christianity the official religion of his empire, such that anyone who refused baptism would die by the sword. Not exactly what Jesus had in mind.

Enter Alcuin of York (ca. 735–804) into Charlemagne's life. Alcuin was generally regarded as "the most learned man anywhere to be found," as his near contemporary Einhard wrote. Alcuin met Charlemagne in 781 after a trip to Rome, and Charlemagne urged him to join his court as a master teacher. He accepted the offer and introduced a liberal arts curriculum of seven subjects to Charlemagne's sons and noble families.

Alcuin was a devout Christian who had served the church in various leadership roles and took exception with the emperor's policy of forcing Christianity on people. Genuine faith, he said, cannot be achieved with a sword. He wrote a strongly worded letter to Charlemagne in 796, asserting, "Faith is a free act of the will, not a forced act. We must appeal to the conscience, not compel it by violence. You can force people to be baptized, but you cannot force them to believe." His argument convinced Charlemagne to abolish the death penalty for unbelievers in 798.

Alcuin is also remembered for developing a more legible style of handwriting and inventing the question mark.

Almighty and merciful God,
Fountain of all goodness,
you know the thoughts of our hearts.
We confess that we have sinned against you,
and done evil in your sight.
Wash us from the stains of our past sins,
and give us grace and power to put away all hurtful things.
Deliver us from the bondage of sin,
that we may bring forth worthy fruits of repentance.

O eternal Light, shine into our hearts.
O eternal Goodness, deliver us from evil.
O eternal Power, be our support.
Eternal Wisdom, scatter the darkness of our ignorance.
Eternal Pity, have mercy on us.
Grant that with all our hearts, and minds, and strength,
we may always seek your face.
In your infinite mercy, bring us into your holy presence.
Strengthen our weakness that,
following in the footsteps of your blessed Son,
we may obtain your mercy,
and enter your promised joy.
Amen.

Theodore the Studite

I still have my "Life is messy" coffee mug. "Life Is Messy" was the title of a series of sermons I preached on Joseph's life from Genesis some years ago. I heard more from my congregation about this sermon series than about any other I had preached. I suspect it's because people closely identified with the "messy" theme.

The life of Theodore the Studite (759–826) certainly qualifies as messy. This highly regarded Byzantine monk was exiled three times! When the Roman emperor Constantine VI divorced his wife to marry her personal assistant, Theodore called him on it, leading to his banishment from a Constantinople monastery—exile #1. He eventually returned, only to lock horns with a second emperor over reinstating the priest who had performed Constantine's wedding; the emperor had Theodore arrested and deported to a remote island—exile #2. He came back, only to tangle with a third emperor over the use of icons in worship. Yep, you guessed it—exile #3. Theodore made the most of his predicaments. He led church reforms in exile and restored monastic virtues of obedience, charity, and chastity to prominence.

You may resonate with this "Life is messy" theme. But while it aptly describes confusing circumstances and tangled relationships, it does not tell the whole story. The tagline "Life is messy" has a biblical sequel: "Life is messy, but God prevails." God prevailed in Joseph's life. God prevailed in Theodore's life. And God prevails in our lives also.

O Lord, who gave your apostles peace,
shed down on us your holy calm.
Gather together with your hand
all those who are scattered,
and bring them like sheep into the fold of your holy church,
through Jesus Christ our Lord.

Strengthen and confirm me,
O Lord, by your cross,
on the rock of faith,
that my mind be not shaken
by the attacks of the enemy.
For you alone are holy.

You know, O Lord,
how many and great are my sins.
You know how often I sin,
from day to day,
from hour to hour,
in the things I do,
and the things I leave undone.
No more, O Lord,
no more, O Lord my God,
will I provoke you.
No more shall my desire be for anything but you,
for you alone are truly loveable.
And if again I offend in anything,
I humbly ask your mercy
to grant me strength
to live in a manner more pleasing to you.
Amen.

Dionysius of Tel Mahre

I don't appreciate it when people label me. I feel constrained by the limits that labels force on me. There is truth to the quote attributed to Søren Kierkegaard, that "once you label me, you negate me."

Born in the small city of Tel Mahre in Syria, Dionysius (d. 845) was elected patriarch of Antioch, the see of the Syriac Orthodox Church, in 818, a position he served in until his death. Syria had already been absorbed into the expanding Muslim empire, which resulted in bad blood between Christians and Muslims. Most of Dionysius's colleagues in the Syriac Orthodox Church regarded Muslims with hostility and disdain. He resolved to stop the bleeding by traveling to Baghdad to seek an audience with the Abbasid caliph al-Ma'mun, chief ruler of the Islamic world. Dionysius introduced himself as a fellow imam, which caught the Islamic leader off guard. Dionysius had done his homework. He was intimately acquainted with the Islamic religion and well versed in Arabic. He sought to find areas of commonality and agreement with al-Ma'mun.

Was it an overreach for Dionysius to call himself an imam? An imam in the classic sense refers to someone who leads prayers in a mosque. Dionysius redeployed Islamic language to describe his similar role in leading prayers for his community. His calculated move paid off. Al-Ma'mun made good on his promise to ensure peace and uphold justice for Christians living in his empire. It was a high-water mark in Muslim-Christian relations.

The story of Dionysius would make a good case study today. Eschew the labels and forgo the stereotypes. Practice civility and love your neighbor. Know what your neighbors believe and seek consensus whenever possible. Agree to disagree.

O God the Father, origin of Divinity,

good beyond all that is good,

fair beyond all that is fair,

in whom are calmness, peace, and concord:

heal the dissensions that divide us from each other,

and bring us back into a unity of love

that may bear some likeness to your divine nature.

And as you are above all things,

make us one by the unanimity of a sound mind,

that through the embrace of charity and the bonds of affection,

we may be spiritually one,

as well in ourselves as in each other,

through that peace of yours that makes all things peaceful,

and through the grace, mercy, and tenderness of your Son, Jesus Christ.

Amen.

Alfred, King of Wessex

Winston Churchill called him "the greatest Englishman ever." He was one of only two English kings awarded the designation "The Great" for extraordinary leadership. He's remembered as the monarch who saved England from Viking invasion, united Saxony (forerunner to modern England), and preserved English as a written language.

Alfred (ca. 848–899) was a king who lived by the principle "I embrace the purpose of God." He carried around with him a notebook of psalms and written prayers, which he prayed often. He prefaced his edition of the English law code with a list of the Ten Commandments from Exodus 20 and various civil laws from Exodus 21–23 to reinforce the commands. Next, he cited Jesus's teachings on the Ten Commandments in his Sermon on the Mount and concluded by referencing their importance to the apostles at the Council of Jerusalem (Acts 15). No other lawbook at that time gave so much credence to biblical teaching. Alfred also translated major portions of the Latin Bible into English as well as major theological works by Augustine and Gregory the Great.

Quick! Forward this post to our elected leaders! We need more politicians like Alfred.

How did he manage to lead his country while caring for his people's spiritual welfare? He lived a highly disciplined life, allocating eight hours each day for rest and food, eight hours for prayer, reading, and writing, and eight hours for his job as king. He placed twenty-four candles in a chapel, each of which burned for one hour. A sexton would alert Alfred to the passage of time at the end of every hour.

Lord God Almighty,
shaper and ruler of all creatures,
we pray for your great mercy,
that you would guide us toward you,
for we cannot find our way.
And guide us to your will, to the need of our soul,
for we cannot do it ourselves.
And make our mind steadfast in your will
and aware of our soul's need.
Strengthen us against the temptations of the devil,
and remove from us all lust and every unrighteousness,
and shield us against our foes, seen and unseen.
Teach us to do your will,
that we may inwardly love you before all things with a pure mind.
For you are our maker and our redeemer,
our help, our comfort, our trust, our hope.
Praise and glory be to you now and forever,
world without end.
Amen.

Anselm of Canterbury

God calls some people in the Bible to assignments not of their own choosing. Take Jonah. God called him to preach repentance to the people of Nineveh. Instead, Jonah booked passage on a cruise ship bound for Tarshish. It took him three days in the belly of a great fish to convince Jonah to cooperate with God's plan.

Anselm of Canterbury (ca. 1033–1109) accepted a call to work unsuited to his own inclinations. He preferred the relative obscurity of monastic life, where he could think, write, and pray. The highly visible job of archbishop of Canterbury didn't interest him. He had no great aspiration to mediate disputes between kings and popes or to intervene with priests whose lives had gone off the rails. He vigorously resisted his appointment and even had to be dragged to the swearing-in ceremony. The bishop's staff signifying his pastoral office had to be forced into his clenched fist.

Anselm finally acquiesced, stating his terms for acceptance, including the recovery of prayer and Scripture meditation as matters of ultimate priority. He ably led the church and turned out an endless supply of fresh theological and philosophical insights. While living in exile for offending King William II, he wrote one of his lasting contributions, *Cur Deus Homo* (Why God Became Man). It's a deep dive into the meaning of the cross, which he interpreted, to put it succinctly, as Jesus's sacrifice that paid humanity's sinful debt to God, thereby opening the way to forgiveness and reconciliation with God.

Anselm rose to become one of the most erudite scholars and original thinkers of the Middle Ages. His famous words "I believe in order to understand" are reflected in one of his prayers from the *Proslogion*.

O Lord my God,
teach my heart where and how it may seek you,
where and how it may find you. . . .
Lord, you are my God,
and yet I have never seen you.
It is you who has made me,
and made me anew,
and who has bestowed on me all the blessings I enjoy,
and yet I still do not know you. . . .
Teach me to seek you,
and reveal yourself to me when I seek you,
for I cannot seek you, except you teach me,
nor find you, except you reveal yourself.
Let me seek you in longing,
let me long for you in seeking;
let me find you in love,
and love you in finding.

Hildegard of Bingen

I first learned about Hildegard of Bingen (ca. 1098–1179) in a *Washington Post* article about beer. This twelfth-century abbess (leader) of a convent in Germany was the first person to document the use of hops in making beer.

I have come to find out that Hildegard was no ordinary nun. She was unique among songwriters of her day for composing both words and music. There are more chants associated with her than with any other songwriter of the Middle Ages. She played the ten-string psaltery (comparable to a dulcimer). She wrote sixty-nine musical compositions, plus the first-ever morality play, complete with eighty-two songs. (The devil is the only one who doesn't sing in Hildegard's play. He only yells and grunts since he cannot produce divine harmony.) She kept an herb garden and became a pioneer of holistic medicine. Her fellow nuns and residents of the wider community consulted her about using herbs and plants to combat illness. She conducted four preaching tours through Germany, speaking primarily to male-dominated audiences, denouncing clergy corruption and urging church reform. No wonder so many divergent groups claim Hildegard as their own.

"Holy persons draw to themselves all that is earthly," Hildegard wrote. Jesus's concern was not only with the hereafter. He summoned followers to promote human flourishing on earth by every means possible.

Jesus Christ, the love that gives love,
You are higher than the highest star.
You are deeper than the deepest sea.
You cherish us as your own family.
You embrace us as your own spouse.
You rule over us as your own subjects.
You welcome us as your dearest friend.
Let all the world worship you.

Holy Spirit, the life that gives life,
You are the cause of all our movements.
You are the salve that purifies our souls.
You are the ointment that heals our wounds.
You are the fire that warms our hearts.
You are the light that guides our feet.
Let all the world praise you.

O eternal God,
Turn us into the arms and hands,
The legs and feet,
Of your beloved Son, Jesus.
You gave birth to us on earth,
To become his living body.
Make us worthy to be his limbs,
And so worthy to share in his eternal bliss.
Let all the world serve you.

Guigo II

It was a hot summer morning in 1150. Guigo II (d. ca. 1188) was working in his garden in a Carthusian monastery in France, harvesting herbs to produce a liqueur called Chartreuse, which Carthusian monks are known for. He was meditating on the story of Jacob's ladder in Genesis 28 when it dawned on him that prayer is like a ladder with four rungs, each rung representing deeper entry into union with God. He had been corresponding with a friend and fellow monk named Gervase about prayer. His seventeen-page letter to Gervase, which came to be known as *The Ladder of Monks: A Letter on the Contemplative Life*, inspired a method of Bible reading and prayer called *lectio divina* (Latin for "spiritual reading") that has instructed believers since the Middle Ages. This prayer exercise consists of four movements, symbolized as rungs on a ladder. The first rung is reading a few verses of Scripture. The second rung is meditating on the verses' deeper meaning. The third rung is praying what the text brings to awareness. And the fourth rung is resting in the quietness of God's promised presence.

Guigo likens these four prayer rungs to eating. Reading puts food in the mouth, meditation chews it, prayer extracts its flavor, and contemplation savors its sweetness. He illustrates this four-step process with a verse from Jesus's Sermon on the Mount: "Blessed are the pure in heart, for they will see God" (Matt. 5:8 NIV). First, he advises Gervase to read the verse slowly and deliberately. Second, he directs him to reflect on its deeper meaning. What does it mean to be blessed? Since Guigo knows his heart is *impure*, he recalls a verse from the Psalms: "Create in me a pure heart, O God, and renew a steadfast spirit within me" (Ps. 51:10 NIV). He imagines what it would be like, as referenced in the latter half of the verse, to see God. Third, he offers the prayer that follows here, and then he concludes with the assurance that God receives our prayers.

Lord, you are not seen except by the pure of heart. I seek by reading and meditating what is true purity of heart and how it may be had, so that with its help I may know you, if only a little. Lord, for long I have meditated in my heart, seeking to see your face. It is the sight of you, Lord, that I have sought; and all the while in my meditation the fire of longing, the desire to know you more fully, has increased. When you break for me the bread of sacred Scripture, you have shown yourself to me in that breaking of bread, and the more I see you, the more I long to see you, no more from without, in the rind [outer layer] of the letter, but within, in the letter's hidden meaning. Nor do I ask this, Lord, because of my own merits, but because of your mercy. I too in my unworthiness confess my sins with the woman who said that "even the little dogs eat the fragments that fall from the table of their masters." So give me, Lord, some pledge of what I hope to inherit, at least one drop of heavenly rain with which to refresh my thirst, for I am on fire with love.

Francis of Assisi

It is commonly called the Prayer of St. Francis. I hate to burst the bubble, but there is no record of the prayer anywhere in Francis's writings. The earliest mention of the prayer associated with Francis is in a 1912 French periodical. The prayer gained popularity during World War I, and by the mid-1920s it was commonly attributed to Francis. While the prayer didn't originate with him, it certainly resembles him.

Francis (ca. 1181–1226) was the consummate peacemaker. His father, a wealthy merchant, urged him to join his lucrative business, but Francis chose the road less traveled. He opposed the militancy of the Crusades and urged a peaceful approach with Muslims. He is legendary in preaching Christ's peace to birds and ravenous wolves. My earliest recollection of St. Francis was my aunt's lawn ornament, complete with birds perched on his shoulders.

Francis founded three religious orders, the most famous of which is the Order of Friars Minor. Included in his "Rule" for the order is the directive "Do not quarrel or argue or judge others; rather, be meek, peaceful, and modest, courteous and humble, speaking honorably to everyone."

While the so-called Prayer of St. Francis has become a sentimental favorite, it calls for a rigorous faith. There is nothing simple or easy about extending mercy to people who malign or criticize us. Only as we contemplate the enormity of God's forgiveness can we grant mercy to others.

Lord, make me an instrument of your peace.
Where there is hatred, let me sow love;
where there is injury, pardon;
where there is doubt, faith;
where there is despair, hope;
where there is darkness, light;
where there is sadness, joy.

O divine Master,
grant that I may not so much seek to be consoled, as to console,
to be understood, as to understand,
to be loved, as to love,
for it is in giving that we receive,
it is in pardoning that we are pardoned,
and it is in dying that we are born to eternal life.

Richard of Chichester

It's not often that a prayer by a medieval bishop becomes the impetus for a pop song, but such is the case with a song from the musical *Godspell*. Who could have imagined that the catchy triplicate rhyme from the refrain of "Day by Day" sung by a motley crew of hippie-looking disciples originated with a thirteenth-century saint?

Richard of Chichester (1197–1253) walked away from a sizable family estate and spurned his family's attempts to arrange for his marriage, instead pursuing a contemplative life. After his studies and his consecration as priest, Richard was elected bishop of Chichester, England, even though King Henry III preferred a candidate who was clueless about theology. Despite repeated attempts by the meddling king to lessen Richard's influence, Richard became an exemplary bishop. His deep spirituality and frugal lifestyle (he wore a hair shirt, practiced a vegetarian diet, and refused to eat off silver) brought much-needed reform to the church in a time of considerable stagnation and corruption.

The prayer for which Richard is most remembered was prayed on his deathbed. Richard's close friend and private confessor, Ralph Bocking, was a Dominican friar who had been called to Richard's bedside in his final moments. He was so enamored with Richard's deathbed prayer that he copied it down and included it in his biography of his departed friend.

With an economy of words, the prayer offers final confession, expresses gratitude for God's mercy, and closes with poetic flourish. In a single sentence, Richard references the importance of Christian doctrine ("know you more clearly"), devotion ("love you more dearly"), and discipleship ("follow you more nearly"). You can tell a lot about people by the way they pray.

Thanks be to thee, O Lord Jesus Christ,
for all the benefits which thou hast given us,
for all the pains and insults which thou hast borne for us.
O most merciful Redeemer, Friend, and Brother,
may we know thee more clearly,
love thee more dearly,
and follow thee more nearly,
for thine own sake.
Amen.

Thomas Aquinas

His family had a cushy job picked out for him. Thomas would become abbot (leader) of a wealthy monastery that had grown lax in its monastic rigor. Thomas Aquinas (ca. 1225–1274) did not share his family's enthusiasm for this prearranged scheme. He aspired to set out for Rome and join the Dominicans, a new order of begging friars. His rich family refused to entertain the idea that Thomas would become a beggar, so his brothers abducted him and brought him home. Thomas was held prisoner in the family castle for a year. They tried to deprogram him, and even went so far as to hire a prostitute to seduce him, but Thomas drove her away with a burning stick. His mother showed him clemency and deliberately left a castle window open so Thomas could escape under the cover of darkness. He traveled to Paris to study with the Dominicans.

Not that he had a promising start. He didn't speak much, so his fellow students thought he was slow and nicknamed him "Dumb Ox." When a Dominican professor, Albertus Magnus, caught wind of the bullying, he exploded: "You call him a dumb ox, but his teaching will one day produce such a bellowing that it will be heard throughout the world."

These words turned out to be prophetic. Thomas Aquinas rose through the ranks to teach theology at the University of Paris and later returned home to Italy as a professor at the University of Naples. Historians regard him as the finest writer and ablest theologian of the Middle Ages. One quote from Aquinas stands out above the rest: "The things we love tell us what we are." How true: we are what we love.

Give me, O Lord, a steadfast heart,
which no unworthy affection may drag downward;
give me an unconquered heart,
which no tribulation can wear out;
give me an upright heart,
which no unworthy purpose may tempt aside.
Bestow upon me also, O Lord my God,
understanding to know you,
diligence to seek you,
wisdom to find you,
and a faithfulness that may finally embrace you.
Amen.

Julian of Norwich

In the final stanza of his poem "Little Gidding," T. S. Eliot writes that "all shall be well and / All manner of thing shall be well," a quote from Julian of Norwich (ca. 1342–ca. 1416). On the surface, Julian's words sound naive and simplistic, yet she lived during a time of incredible turmoil. She endured three waves of the bubonic plague that decimated half her town, a peasant revolt, and her own life-threatening illness. She became deathly ill at age thirty and received sixteen distinct visions from Christ upon her recovery. Such visions are outside my frame of reference, so I press on.

Julian lived as an anchorite for twenty years. OK, I had to look this word up. An anchorite is someone who withdraws from society to live a prayer-saturated, ascetic life. She never left her room attached to a church for twenty years! Three windows provided her with her only contact with others: a window open to the sanctuary to participate in worship, a window accessible to servant quarters to arrange for food and necessities, and a window open to the outside world, to offer townspeople spiritual counsel. Why would anyone want to live this way?

She wrote *Revelations of Divine Love* as a prayer exercise. She didn't intend it for publication, but it was found in her room upon her death and printed posthumously, the first book in English by a female writer. She addressed two common struggles in her writing: impatience and despair. When we become impatient for prayers to be answered, she observed, God intends for us to wait for a better time. When we are tempted with despair, she observed, feelings aren't the final determinant of God's love for us.

One thing we can take away from Julian is a resolute assurance of God's infinite love. Don't underestimate God's love. Scripture testifies that God, in the end, will make things right again. All things will be put right by Christ. We join with the apostle Paul in declaring that nothing "will be able to separate us from the love of God that is in Christ Jesus our Lord" (Rom. 8:38–39 NIV).

God, of your goodness,
give me yourself,
for you are enough for me.
I cannot properly ask anything less
to be worthy of you.
If I were to ask less,
I should always be in want,
for in you alone do I have all.

Catherine of Siena

Jesus was the epitome of contemplation in action. He was a model contemplative, withdrawing from people at regular intervals for intentional prayer. Yet he was also an activist, healing the sick and proclaiming the kingdom of God. His rich inner life directed his dynamic outer life. Separating contemplation from action leads to a distortion in either direction. Contemplation without action leads to self-absorption. Action without contemplation leads to burnout.

Catherine of Siena (1347–1380) sought to balance contemplation with action. She was a contemplative of the highest order, rigorous in her practice of prayer, meditation, and fasting. Her principal writing, the *Dialogue*, reveals an intimate conversation between her soul and God. She discusses with Jesus weighty matters like the reform of his church and the conversion of the world. Yet her life with Christ also involved "blood," "sweat," and "tears," favorite terms of Catherine's.

At a time when religious vocations for women were limited to the convent, Catherine had the ear of popes and princes. She served as a key adviser to Popes Gregory XI and Urban VI, addressing them in letters affectionately as "Babbo" (Daddy) instead of the formal "Your Highness." She traveled throughout Italy urging reform for clergy and reconciling warring factions. She was sent on several vital diplomatic missions. Many of her four hundred letters that survive demonstrate her activism in many directions.

Was Catherine successful in merging contemplation with action? Her influence was considerable, yet she also died prematurely after years of extreme fasting. Whether she suffered from anorexia remains a matter of scholarly debate. Regardless, her recorded prayers display the depth of her spirituality and her genuine seeking after God.

You, eternal Trinity, are a deep sea: the more I enter you, the more I discover, and the more I discover, the more I seek you. You are insatiable, you in whose depth the soul is sated yet remains always hungry for you, thirsty for you, eternal Trinity, longing to see you with the light in your light. . . .

You, eternal Trinity, are a craftsman; and I your handiwork have come to know that you are in love with the beauty of what you have made, since you made of me a new creation in the blood of your Son.

O abyss! O eternal Godhead! O deep sea! What more could you have given me than the gift of your very self?

You are a fire always burning but never consuming; you are a fire consuming in your heat all the soul's selfish love; you are a fire lifting all chill and giving light. In your light you have made me know your truth: you are that light beyond all light who gives the mind's eye supernatural light in such fullness and perfection that you bring clarity even to the light of faith. In that faith I see that my soul has life, and in that light receives you who are Light.

Thomas à Kempis

Donald Jackson has been called the world's foremost calligrapher. Saint John's University in Collegeville, Minnesota, commissioned him to handwrite and illustrate the entire Bible. Don't feel sorry for the guy. He claimed it was his dream job. He started the project in 1998 and finished it in May 2011. That's thirteen years of copying 1,110-plus pages with quill and ink. Before the invention of the Gutenberg press in 1440, all Bibles were copied this way, and monks at Benedictine monasteries did most of the heavy lifting. It was painstaking, tedious work.

Thomas Haemmerlein (ca. 1380–1471), better known as Thomas à Kempis (after his native town of Kempen, Germany), copied the entire Bible by hand into Latin four times. Four times! Somehow he also found time to write one of the definitive works on the Christian life, *The Imitation of Christ*. He was given the assignment at his Dutch monastery to write a manual for novice monks. He wrote four booklets of instruction and stated his purpose in the first book: "We must imitate Christ's life and his ways. . . . Let it be the most important thing we do." He singled out humility as the most important Christian virtue. "If you are to learn something that will help you," he wrote, "learn to see yourself as God sees you and not as you see yourself in the distorted mirror of your own self-importance."

The Imitation of Christ is one of the most-sold and most-translated books in human history. John Wesley called it the best summary of the Christian life he ever read. One quote attributed to Thomas is a personal favorite: "Without the way, there is no going; without the truth, there is no knowing; without the life, there is no living."

The following prayer is an excerpt from *The Imitation of Christ*.

Grant that nothing in the world might be as important to me as you are, and for your sake grant that I may serve you with deep humility and love, caring little for recognition and honor. Grant above all else, that I may rest in you and that my heart may find peace in you. You are the heart's true peace; you are its only rest. Apart from you, everything is hard and uneasy. Only in this peace that is you, highest and eternal Good, do I find sleep and take my rest. Amen.

Girolamo Savonarola

Active in Florence, Italy, Girolamo Savonarola (1452–1498) was a Dominican friar who called the medieval Roman Catholic Church to account for its moral corruption. There have been plenty of virtuous popes in church history, but Pope Alexander VI wasn't one of them. He bought his way into the papacy and had several mistresses, by whom he fathered four children. Girolamo denounced the pope's hypocrisy in no uncertain terms and demanded moral reform. The pope tried to appease him by offering him the position of cardinal. He refused, and the pope ordered him to come to Rome. Girolamo knew it was a ploy, so he replied that he wasn't feeling well. No more preaching, the pope ordered. Savonarola obliged for a time yet started preaching again. The pope promptly excommunicated him. In pre-Reformation times, if a priest was excommunicated, it meant he couldn't administer the Lord's Supper. And if you couldn't receive Holy Communion, you were unlikely to go to heaven. The people turned on Girolamo, resulting in his arrest and eventual execution.

In 1498, while in prison, he composed a meditation on Psalm 51 titled *Infelix ego* (Alas, wretched man that I am). Psalm 51 is David's penitential prayer after coming to terms with his adultery and murder. Girolamo had just been tortured on the rack and, unable to withstand, had recanted his prophecies of divine judgment. Devastated by his personal weakness, he prayed earnestly for forgiveness and petitioned God for a clean heart.

While we might regard him as too hard on himself, his meditation endures as a model of contrition. The Reformer Martin Luther found inspiration in "that godly man of Florence" and published Girolamo's *Prison Meditation* on Psalm 51, in which is included the following prayer.

Create a clean heart in me, O God:
a humble heart,
a meek heart,
a peaceful heart
a benevolent heart,
a devout heart,
a heart that does harm to no one,
that does not repay evil for evil
but overcomes evil with good,
that loves you above all things,
thinks always about you,
speaks about you,
gives you thanks,
delights in hymns and spiritual songs,
and has its citizenship in heaven.
Amen.

Thomas More

Lawyers have been the punchline of jokes since the time of Shakespeare. According to one Stanford law professor, 60 percent of Americans regard lawyers as greedy while only 20 percent regard them as honest and compassionate.

Thomas More (1478–1535) was a reputable lawyer in his day. He gave serious consideration to becoming a monk but sensed his true calling in the legal profession. He worked as a high-ranking adviser to King Henry VIII and represented the English monarch on several important diplomatic missions. He became Speaker of the House of Commons and lord chancellor in 1529, second in authority to the king. King Henry VIII had married his late brother's wife, Catherine of Aragon. When she failed to produce a male heir to the throne, Henry petitioned the church to have his marriage annulled. He cited as biblical justification an obscure passage about a man who married his brother's wife and became cursed and childless (Lev. 20:21). When Henry failed to gain church support for his annulment, he manipulated the legal process to become head of a new institution, the Church of England, thereby making it possible to divorce Catherine and marry Anne Boleyn.

Thomas resigned his post as chancellor and refused to attend Henry's wedding and Anne's coronation. Henry pressured Parliament to pass the Act of Supremacy, giving him official status as head of the church. When Thomas refused to sign the act, he was imprisoned for fifteen months, during which time he wrote some of his most penetrating works of Christian theology. He was found guilty of treason in a mock trial and executed in 1535. His final words before death are instructive: "The king's good servant, but God's first."

Protestants don't always give Thomas More his due, given his testy letter-writing challenges to Martin Luther over disrupting church unity and undermining its seven sacraments. But surely his integrity as a lawyer and his impactful prayers have much to offer Protestants and Catholics alike.

Glorious God, . . . give me your grace to amend my life and to have an eye to my end without grudge of death, which to them that die in you, good Lord, is but the gate to a wealthy life. . . .

O glorious God, all sinful fear, all sinful sorrow and pensiveness, all sinful hope, all sinful mirth and gladness take from me. . . .

Almighty God, take from me all vanity, all appetites for my own praise, all envy, covetousness, overindulgence, sloth, and lasciviousness, all wrathful affections, all appetites for revenge, all desire for or delight in other folks' harm, all pleasure in provoking any person to wrath and anger. . . .

And give me, good Lord, a humble, lowly, quiet, peaceable, patient, charitable, kind, tender, and compassionate mind with all my works, and all my words, and all my thoughts, to have a taste of you, holy, blessed Spirit.

Give me, good Lord, a full faith, a firm hope, and a fervent charity, a love for you far exceeding my love of self. May I love nothing to your displeasure, but everything in order to you. . . .

The things, good Lord, that I pray for, give me your grace to labor for. Amen.

Martin Luther

The Protestant Reformer Martin Luther (1483–1546) was sitting in a barber's chair in Wittenberg, Germany, one day in spring 1535 when his barber, Peter Baskendorf, asked, "Dr. Luther, how do you pray?" Martin took his question seriously. He went home and composed a thirty-four-page response, later published as *A Simple Way to Pray*. Martin cautioned his friend to guard against thinking, "Wait a little. I will pray in an hour. I must attend to this or that." He advocated setting aside regular times for prayer, making it "the first business of the day and the last at night." He urged Peter to devote to prayer the same focus he'd give to a man receiving a shave or a haircut. If a barber allowed his eyes and mind to wander, he could cut a customer's nose or even his throat.

Martin began his time of prayer with Scripture meditation, to "warm his heart to the things of God." He often prayed the Psalms, which John Calvin, his Reformed colleague, called "an anatomy of all parts of the soul." He also commended music as an aid to prayer and once arranged for a composer to set his favorite psalms to music. Martin incorporated the Lord's Prayer into his daily routine, praying it "once and more slowly a second time," pausing at each petition to add his own reflections in prayer.

Concerned that his friend Philip Melanchthon was ascribing too much piety to him, in 1521 Martin confessed to Philip in a letter that "I sit here like a fool and hardened in leisure, pray little, do not sigh for the church of God, yet burn in a big fire of my untamed body. In short, I should be ardent in spirit, but I am ardent in the flesh, in lust, in laziness, leisure, and sleepiness. . . . Already eight days have passed in which I have written nothing, in which I have not prayed or studied." Take heart, my friend. If this great Reformer struggled with prayer, there's hope for folks like us who chastise ourselves for being intermittent and inconsistent about prayer.

Behold, Lord, an empty vessel that needs to be filled. My Lord, I am weak in faith; strengthen me. I am cold in heart; warm me and make me fervent that my love may go out to my neighbor. I do not have a strong and firm faith; at times I doubt and am unable to trust you altogether. O Lord, help me. Strengthen my faith and trust in you. . . . I am poor; you are rich. I am a sinner; you are upright. With me, there is an abundance of sin; in you there is the fullness of righteousness. Therefore, I will remain with you, of whom I can receive, but to whom I may not give. Amen.

Ulrich Zwingli

The Swiss Reformation began as a dispute over smoked sausage. It was called the Affair of the Sausages. I kid you not! On March 9, 1522, a dozen men gathered at the home of the printer Christopher Froschauer for an evening meal. Ulrich Zwingli (1484–1531) was there, priest of a church in Zurich. Catholic law forbade eating meat during Lent. But Christopher served a meal with two smoked sausages cut up in the main course, in deliberate defiance of church law. Ulrich did not partake of the meal, but he believed the provocation could be justified theologically. Christopher was arrested and sent to jail.

Ulrich preached a sermon two weeks later titled "Regarding the Choice and Freedom of Foods." He appealed to Christians to exercise their freedom of conscience related to fasting. Since there is no biblical law against eating meat during Lent, transgressing such a rule cannot be considered a sin. Ulrich said in his sermon, "If the spirit of your belief leads you thus, then fast, but grant also your neighbor the privilege of Christian liberty."

After Christopher was released from prison, he printed Ulrich's sermon. A Catholic bishop sent a delegation to put Ulrich in his place. Ulrich put forward sixty-seven articles for public debate, which caught the delegation off guard. He argued that Scripture, not tradition, was the final determinant in any church dispute. The city council sided with Ulrich, and the Reformation principle of *sola scriptura* (Scripture alone) took hold in Switzerland.

Ulrich leads us in prayer to hear, understand, believe, and follow God's word.

Living God, help us to hear your holy Word with open hearts so that we may truly understand; and, understanding, that we may believe; and, believing, that we may follow you in all faithfulness and obedience, seeking your honor and glory in all that we do. Through Christ, our Lord. Amen.

Thomas Cranmer

Courage and cowardice can exist in the same person. I can attest to it. I alternate between being a wimp and having a brave heart. I recognize a similar tendency in Thomas Cranmer (1489–1556), a leader of the Protestant Reformation. He orchestrated the writing of the 1549 Book of Common Prayer, still the primary worship resource for Anglican churches.

Under pressure from Queen Mary I's henchmen, Thomas signed a statement renouncing many of the Protestant convictions that had defined his ministry. The queen (Bloody Mary) wanted him dead but first wanted him to announce his recantation publicly, for which purpose he was led from prison to St. Mary's Church. He carried the script of his approved remarks yet had also tucked a revised speech in the lining of his coat. He began as expected but deviated to read from his revised speech and renounce his earlier recantations: "I come to the great thing that troubles my conscience more than any other thing that I ever said or did in my life: and that is, the setting abroad of writings contrary to the truth, which here now I renounce and refuse, as things written with my hand contrary to the truth which I thought in my heart, written for fear of death, and to save my life." He said further that if he should be burned at the stake, his right hand would be the first to be destroyed, since it had signed his recantation. Then, for good measure, he denounced the pope.

His enemies rushed forward, carried him away, and burned him at the stake. He offered his right hand to the flames with the words "the hand hath offended" and prayed at the last, "Lord Jesus, receive my spirit." It was courage when it counted.

We join together in a prayer of confession from the Book of Common Prayer, which Thomas edited.

Almighty and most merciful Father, we have erred and strayed from your ways like lost sheep. We have followed too much the devices and desires of our own hearts. We have offended against your holy laws. We have left undone those things which we ought to have done, and we have done those things which we ought not to have done, and there is no health in us. O Lord, have mercy upon us, miserable offenders. Spare those, O God, who confess their faults. Restore those who are penitent, according to your promises declared to all people through Christ Jesus our Lord. And grant, most merciful Father, for his sake, that we may hereafter live a godly, righteous, and sober life, to the glory of your holy name. Amen.

Martin Bucer

John Calvin was kicked out of his church in Geneva. His friend, Martin Bucer (1491–1551), reached out and invited him to Strasbourg, France. Martin and his wife, Elizabeth, were church reformers like John. Martin had been in training to become a Dominican friar, and Elizabeth was previously a nun. John moved into their home and observed that he had never seen a happier marriage. He said, "In his [Martin's] family, during the entire time I saw not the least account of offense but only ground for edification." John was thirty-one and single. Pastor Martin, who was eighteen years his senior, became his mentor. He helped John Calvin see how his uncompromising attitudes in Geneva had caused needless discord.

Martin made it possible for John Calvin to pastor a church of French exiles living in Strasbourg. John rented a large house near Martin and turned it into a dormitory for students, hoping to recoup expenses. He didn't! He hired a housekeeper with a bad temper who drove boarders away and annoyed him as he edited his *Institutes of the Christian Religion*. "You need a wife," Martin told him. John agreed, so Martin and friends formed a search committee to find a wife for John. The first three candidates didn't pass muster with John, but the fourth one, Idelette, won the marriage sweepstakes. Martin urged John to go back to Geneva when the church extended an invitation for him to return. John served the Genevan church with distinction for twenty-three years and became a Reformation stalwart.

Martin Bucer put himself out for John Calvin. If it had not been for him, there might not have been a John Calvin. We join with Martin in praying to discern God's gracious will for our lives.

Almighty, gracious Father, forasmuch as our whole salvation depends upon our true understanding of your holy Word, grant that our hearts, being freed from worldly affairs, may hear and apprehend your holy Word with all diligence and faith, that we may rightly discern your gracious will, cherish it, and live by it with all earnestness, to your praise and honor, through our Lord Jesus Christ. Amen.

John Calvin

The Reformation leaders Martin Luther and John Calvin (1509–1564) never met in person. When Martin nailed his Ninety-Five Theses to the church door in Wittenberg, John was eight years old. John sent a letter to Martin through a mutual friend, Philip Melanchthon, that was never delivered. Philip wrote to John, "I have not given your letter to Doctor Martin, as he looks at such things with suspicion." Martin was touchy and weary as he neared the end of his life.

The temperaments of these two Reformers were poles apart. Martin Luther said of himself, "I am rough, boisterous, stormy, and belligerent. I was born to fight against monsters and demons." He was outgoing and extroverted, a true "people person." John Calvin, by contrast, was a classic introvert (I'd wager an INTJ on the Myers-Briggs scale). He described himself as "shy and timid." He had deep respect for "Father Luther" yet described him as "immoderately ardent and violent in character." Martin admired John yet also wrote that he was "educated but strongly suspected of the error of the Sacramentarians," a reference to their dispute over the Lord's Supper.

John Calvin following in Martin Luther's footsteps was surely an act of God. Martin functioned as pioneer and trailblazer, the heart of the Reformation. John was its head, the scholar who provided this fledgling movement with theological rigor and depth. Despite their differences, they shared a deep commitment to God in prayer. John devoted one hundred pages of his *Institutes of the Christian Religion* to prayer, which he describes as "intimate conversation with God." He wrote that God's very character gives us every assurance that God hears and answers prayer. Martin's references to prayer permeate John's writings. He consistently advocated that prayer be frequent, bold, honest, and forthright.

The following prayer is a morning prayer by John Calvin.

My God, Father and Savior, since you have been pleased to give me the grace to come through the night to the present day, now grant that I may employ it entirely in your service, so that all my works may be to the glory of your name and the edification of my neighbors. As you have been pleased to make your sun shine upon the earth to give us bodily light, grant the light of your Spirit to illumine my understanding and my heart. And because it means nothing to begin well if one does not persevere, I ask that you continue to increase your grace in me until you have led me into full communion with your Son, Jesus Christ our Lord, who is the true Sun of our souls, shining day and night, eternally and without end. Hear me, merciful Father, by our Lord Jesus Christ. Amen.

John Bradford

Have you ever heard a speaker deliver a message that seemed intended just for you? As John Bradford (1510–1555) listened to a sermon by Hugh Latimer, he was seized with remorse. Hugh, a fellow Reformer, made an impassioned appeal to make restitution for things falsely gotten. John was cut to the heart and resolved to make amends. His former boss, Sir John Harrington, managed money in support of King Henry VIII's army. Some of the money intended for the army found its way into Sir John's pocket. It's unclear what part John Bradford played in the scheme. Likely, he knew about it but said nothing. He brought the matter to Sir John after hearing the sermon. Sir John was reluctant to pay the money back, but John persisted, offering cash from the sale of his father's estate to make it happen. Sir John agreed to the deal and the money was repaid. Character is what we are when no one is looking.

John Bradford became famous in England for his personal integrity. He was later arrested for seditious preaching when Queen Mary went on her rampage against Protestants. John was found guilty in a mock trial and burned at the stake. He said to a fellow martyr moments before the wood was lit, "Be of good comfort, brother, for we shall have a merry supper with our Lord this night."

What John wrote about prayer is a keeper: "Prayer is the simple, unfeigned, humble, and ardent opening of the heart before God in which we either ask for things needful or give thanks for benefits received."

O Lord Jesus!
I beseech thy goodness. . . .
Draw me out of myself into thee, my Lord God,
and grant that thy love may recover again thy grace to me,
to increase and make perfect in me that which is wanting,
to raise up in me that which is fallen,
to restore to me that which I have lost,
and to quicken in me that which is dead and should live,
so that I may become conformable unto thee
in all my life and conversation,
thou dwelling in me and I in thee,
my heart being supplied with thy grace,
and settled in thy faith forever.
Amen.

Teresa of Ávila

Some Christians hear God's voice in visions and experience God's presence through dreams. So-called mystical Christians are people who not only think great thoughts about God but also experience God deep in the soul.

Teresa of Ávila (1515–1582) was a sixteenth-century Spanish mystic who has much to teach Christians today about the practice of prayer. She desired early in life to join a convent, but her father objected. If a woman in those days desired to serve God as a full-time vocation, the only avenue available to her was to join a convent. Teresa prevailed on her father to enter a Carmelite order of nuns at age twenty. By her own admission, she was an ordinary, not-so-devout nun until age thirty-nine, when she entered into a profound season of prayer.

As she matured in her spiritual life, other nuns asked her for help in learning how to pray. She wrote *The Way of Perfection* to introduce various ways of vocal, mental, and silent praying. The book for which she is most known, *The Interior Castle*, is a deep dive into the spiritual journey meant to lead believers into ultimate union with God. While her writing is dense and sometimes hard to follow, her insights into prayer are worth the effort. She wrote, for example, "You pay God a compliment by asking great things of him." Her last words, spoken as a prayer, are memorable: "The hour I have longed for has come. It is time to meet one another."

It would be a mistake to label Teresa only as a contemplative. She founded fourteen monasteries in Spain to revitalize and expand the mercy mission of the church.

The following prayer of hers comes from her spiritual autobiography, *The Book of My Life*.

O my Beloved! It appears that you are determined to save me. May it please you do to it! You have already poured such a bounty of blessings upon me. What I don't understand is why you have allowed this dwelling of my soul, where you have chosen to live, to remain in such a terrible mess. It is not for my own advantage that I ask, but for your honor and glory. . . . Blessed are you, O Lord, who have put up with me for so long! Amen.

Jane Grey

I once officiated at a double wedding for two sisters who wanted to marry their respective grooms on the same day. That's nothing! Lady Jane Grey (1537–1554) was married at age sixteen to Lord Guildford Dudley in a *triple* wedding!

Jane became queen of England in the same year she married. They called her the "Nine-Day Queen" because that's how long her reign lasted. She was replaced by her half sister Mary, whose nickname, Bloody Mary, tells you something about her style of leadership. The group responsible for royal appointments quickly changed allegiances to Mary, the result of shady religious dealings. Jane the Protestant was replaced with Mary the Catholic. Jane was arrested and charged with high treason, which carried the sentence of death. Her execution was postponed three days to give her a second chance to convert to medieval Catholicism. How thoughtful! Jane didn't buckle; she stayed the course.

You get a sense of Jane's deep convictions in a letter she wrote in prison to her fourteen-year-old sister Katherine, which reads in part, "Live or die, that by death you may enter into eternal life, and then enjoy the life that Christ has gained for you by his death. Don't think that just because you are now young your life will be long, because young or old, as God wills." Need I remind you, Jane is sixteen. Jane carried to her execution a collection of prayers from fourth-century Christian leaders like Jerome, Augustine, and Ambrose, all saints in the Catholic tradition. She entered the following original prayer into her journal shortly before her execution.

O merciful God, consider my misery, best known unto Thee, and be unto me a strong tower of defense. I humbly entreat Thee, suffer me not to be tempted above my power, but either be a deliverer out of this great misery, or give me grace patiently to bear Thy heavy hand and sharp correction. . . .

Give me grace to await Thy leisure, and patiently to bear Thy works, assuredly knowing Thou wilt deliver me, when it shall please Thee, not doubting or mistrusting Thy goodness toward me; for Thou knowest better what is good for me than I do: therefore do with me in all things what Thou wilt. . . .

Only in the meantime, arm me, I beseech Thee, with Thine armor, that I may stand fast, . . . above all things taking to me the shield of faith, . . . praying always that I may refer myself wholly to Thy will, abiding Thy pleasure, and comforting myself in those troubles that it shall please Thee to send me, seeing such troubles are profitable for me; and I am assuredly persuaded that it cannot but be well.

Hear me, O merciful Father, for his sake, Thou who wouldst be a sacrifice for my sins; to whom with Thee and the Holy Spirit, be all honor and glory. Amen.

Johannes Kepler

Johannes Kepler (1571–1630) was an astronomer who believed God created order in the universe for us to understand and put to good use. So what's the problem? The leading scholars of his day were convinced the earth was the center of the solar system—that the earth was stationary and the sun and other planets revolved around it. Johannes was one of the few astronomers who embraced the Copernican view that the earth and other planets orbited around the sun. It was considered radical, even heretical, to hold such a divergent view. Also in his day, there was no clear delineation between astronomy and astrology. But Johannes had little use for astrology. In his words, "Astrology is the foolish little daughter to mother astronomy."

Johannes's original plan was to become a Lutheran pastor, but he found his true calling in his pioneering work as an astronomer. He wrote, "I had the intention of being a theologian, . . . but now I sense how God is, by my endeavors, also glorified in astronomy, for 'the heavens declare the glory of God.'" His three principles of planetary motion, called Kepler's laws, added credence to the Copernican view. He also speculated that there must be some force created by the sun causing the motion of the planets; Isaac Newton later utilized his work by identifying gravity as the force Johannes imagined.

Johannes was frequently quoted as saying in his study of God's universe, "O Lord, I am thinking thy thoughts after thee." When a pastor asked him at the end of his life about his hope of salvation, he answered, "I believe only and alone in the merit of Jesus Christ. In him is all refuge and solace."

Thank you, my Creator and God,
for giving me such a delight in your universe,
this ecstasy when I look at your handiwork.
As far as my finite spirit has been able to comprehend,
I have shared with others the glory of your works
and your infinity. . . .
If anything I have said misrepresents you,
or if at any time I have sought my own glory,
graciously forgive me.
Amen.

George Herbert

His friends said the job was "beneath him." It was a modest assignment for someone of George Herbert's (1593–1633) exceptional abilities and extensive background. He was a gifted scholar, serving as spokesman for the prestigious Trinity College in Cambridge, England. He had been a respected member of the British Parliament, yet he couldn't shake that what he really wanted to be was a pastor.

He was called to St. Andrew's, a country church in Bemerton, Wiltshire. His congregation was made up of common laborers, and most were illiterate. "I will labor to make it honorable," he said to dubious friends, referring to the task of training uneducated people in a rural church. That he did! He rebuilt the dilapidated sanctuary with his own money. He fed the poor, visited the sick, and sought to reconcile feuding neighbors. He became known around town affectionately as "Holy Mr. Herbert." He and his wife, Jane, had no biological children, but they adopted three orphaned nieces. He served the church for three years before tuberculosis claimed his life in 1633. He is buried under the church altar.

On his deathbed, George gave to a friend a manuscript of poems that he had been writing and revising in his spare time. His friend arranged to have the poems published in a collection titled *The Temple*. George regarded poetry as a type of preaching. "A verse may find him, who a sermon flies," he wrote. People are still reading his poetry, now more than ever. One poem in *The Temple* is simply titled "Prayer." You may want to check it out. He utilizes twenty-six images for prayer in just fourteen lines. In one image, he describes prayer as pilgrimage —life in journey with God.

You can detect George's heart for God in the following prayer, taken from *The Country Parson*, a handbook he wrote on pastoral care.

You, Lord, are patience, and pity, and sweetness, and love; therefore, we sons of men are not consumed. You have exalted your mercy above all things, and have made our salvation, not our punishment, your glory; so that then where sin abounded, not death but grace superabounded. Accordingly, where we had sinned beyond any help in heaven or earth, then you said, "Lo, I come!" Then did the Lord of life, unable of himself to die, contrive to do it. He took flesh, he wept, he died; for his enemies he died, even for those that derided him then, and still despise him. Blessed Savior! Many waters cannot quench your love, nor can any pit overwhelm it! But though the streams of your blood were coursing through darkness, grave, and hell, yet by these your conflicts and seemingly hazards did you arise triumphant, and therein made us victorious. Amen.

John Cosin

The English king Charles I married the French princess Henrietta Maria in 1625. She was fifteen and he was twenty-four. She was not Charles's first choice, and their marriage was full of high drama, but that's a story for another day. When Henrietta Maria became queen, she asked Charles on behalf of her court for a printed resource on the various hours of prayer. It was a common practice of Christians in those days, and still is in many Christian traditions, to engage in morning, noon, afternoon, and evening prayers. King Charles summoned John Cosin (1594–1672), a well-respected theologian and Anglican priest, to fulfill his wife's request. I'm trying to imagine an American president requesting a similar prayer guide for use by elected civil servants! Given the current political rancor, it's not a bad idea, but I digress.

John devoted three months to writing his *Collection of Private Devotions*. He included written prayers already in circulation as well as others composed by his own hand. He chose various psalm readings as an aid to prayer and wrote new hymns for use in worship, plus translated others from Latin into English. One such hymn, "Come, Holy Ghost, Our Souls Inspire," is still in circulation today. A prayer from his *Collection of Private Devotions* follows here. I marvel at his ability to express so much in so few words. He offers everything to God in prayer.

Be thou a light unto mine eyes,
music to mine ears,
sweetness to my taste,
and full contentment to my heart.
Be thou my sunshine in the day,
my food at the table,
my repose in the night,
my clothing in nakedness,
and my succor in all necessities.

Lord Jesus, I give thee my body,
my soul, my substance,
my fame, my friends,
my liberty, and my life.
Dispose of me, and all that is mine,
as it seems best to thee,
and to the glory of thy blessed name.
Amen.

John Milton

John Milton (1608–1674) was nearing the end of his eventful life. He felt as if he had one last poem in him. He rose each morning at 5:00 a.m., meditated on his Hebrew Bible for an hour, and offered the day in prayer. (John had learned ancient Hebrew as a child, and as a fifteen-year-old, he had translated Psalm 114 from Hebrew into English.) After breakfast, he worked until noon on the poem *Paradise Lost*. He took a break for lunch and played the organ and viola for recreation. He then resumed labors on his epic poem until the evening meal.

I didn't know until recently that John Milton didn't actually write *Paradise Lost*. He dictated it. He was blind by this time, so he spoke his text to scribes, primarily his daughters. He spoke nearly eleven thousand lines of *Paradise Lost*, then followed it with the sequel, *Paradise Regained*. What drove John to do this? Undoubtedly, part of his motivation was self-serving. He wrote his magnum opus to be remembered. It was his way of coping with his loss of sight and his growing disenchantment with British politics. But he also sought, in his own words, "to justify the ways of God to men."

Milton was a flawed man. He was difficult to live with and hard on Roman Catholics. He was a restless Puritan, trying to make sense of essential biblical themes, yet he also sought to live as a committed follower of Christ. The following prayer is adapted from the opening stanza of *Paradise Lost*.

Holy Spirit of God,
who prefers before all temples
the upright heart and pure,
instruct us in all truth.
What is dark, illumine;
what is low, raise and support;
what is shallow, deepen;
that every chapter in our lives
may witness to your power
and justify the ways of God to men.
In the name of Jesus, giver of all grace.
Amen.

Jeremy Taylor

What became of the virtue of humility? It is being passed over today in total silence. Pride, which used to be ranked as one of the "seven deadly sins," has kicked humility to the curb. Humility has evolved into a weakness or character flaw.

In seventeenth-century England, humility was regarded as an essential Christian virtue. Jeremy Taylor (1613–1667) called humility "the great jewel of the Christian religion." This influential Anglican priest wrote a definitive guide in 1650 on how to live with humility in the presence of God. He titled it *The Rule and Exercises for Holy Living*. Incidentally, he wrote a sequel called—are you ready for this?—*The Rule and Exercises for Holy Dying*. Today's death-denying culture would probably lobby to have it banned from library shelves.

Jeremy devoted a major section of his *Holy Living* book to the practice of humility. He identified nineteen rules for how to promote humility. Rules like "Never say anything directly or indirectly that will evoke praise" and "Do not constantly try to excuse all your faults" and "Be content when you see or hear that others are doing well in their jobs and with their income, even when you are not." (You can google "Rules for the Grace of Humility" for the entire list.) His comments on humility remind me of something Rick Warren wrote in *The Purpose Driven Life*: "Humility is not thinking less of yourself; it is thinking of yourself less."

The following prayer from Jeremy Taylor's *Holy Living* asks God to show us our rightful place.

Guide us, Lord,
in all the changes and varieties of the world,
that we may have evenness and tranquility of spirit,
that we may not grumble in adversity,
nor grow proud in prosperity,
but in serene faith surrender our souls
to your most divine will,
through Jesus Christ our Lord.
Amen.

Blaise Pascal

Blaise Pascal (1623–1662) spent the first thirty-one years of his life doing what brilliant people do. He formulated Pascal's theorem of geometry at sixteen. He created the first mechanical calculator at nineteen. He invented the syringe, the hydraulic press, and a whole lot more. For good measure, he also formulated the theory of probability.

Everything changed on the night of November 23, 1654. He called it his "night of fire." For two hours, he had an experience with the transforming love of God that changed the course of his life. He was reading John 17, where Jesus prays before giving himself over to be crucified. As Blaise read, the room filled with God's presence. He wrote on parchment a description of what happened and sewed it into the lining of his coat to be reminded of it. For the remaining years of his life, Blaise devoted himself to writing various defenses of Christianity. His last work, still in fragmentary form, was published after his death as *Pensées* (Thoughts).

I'm intrigued by what he writes about the paradoxical nature of people. Human beings exhibit both "greatness and wretchedness." People are capable of inexplicable goodness as well as unspeakable atrocities. How can we be at one and the same time Dr. Jekyll and Mr. Hyde? Blaise concludes that Christianity offers the best explanation for the human predicament. We are great because we are created in the image of God, and we are wretched because we have fallen from God's grace.

This prayer from Blaise typifies his keen mind and warm heart.

Lord, let us do little things
as though they were great,
because of the majesty of Jesus Christ,
who does them in us and lives our life,
and let us do the greatest things
as though they were little and easy,
because of your omnipotence.
Amen.

John Flavel

A man entered a bookstore in 1673 looking for plays (think *Romeo and Juliet*). The owner, Mr. Boulder, suggested the man read John Flavel's book *Keeping the Heart*. The man glanced at the title, thumbed through the pages, and handed the book back to Mr. Boulder. He remarked that he would rather burn the suggested book than read it. Mr. Boulder pressed him further, saying that if he didn't like the book, he would gladly refund him his money. The man bought the book and returned to the store a month later. "Sir, I thank you for putting this book into my hands. It has saved my soul; blessed be God that I ever came into your shop." The man proceeded to buy a hundred more copies to give to friends.

The book's author, John Flavel (ca. 1630–1691), was a Puritan preacher and noted author. *Keeping the Heart* takes its title from Proverbs 4:23: "Keep thy heart with all diligence; for out of it are the issues of life" (KJV). John wrote in the foreword, "The greatest difficulty in conversion is to win the heart to God, and the greatest difficulty after conversion is to keep the heart with God." His book teaches in practical terms how to develop the habit of daily communion with God. He wrote, "All I beg for is that you will step aside a little more often to talk with God and your own heart."

This prayer is from John Flavel's sermon "Of the Solemn Consecration of the Mediator," published in 1671 in the compilation *The Fountain of Life*.

Lord, the condemnation was yours,
that the justification might be mine.
The agony was yours,
that the victory might be mine.
The pain was yours,
and the ease mine.
The stripes were yours,
and the healing balm issuing from them mine.
The vinegar and gall were yours,
that the honey and sweet might be mine.
The curse was yours,
that the blessing might be mine.
The crown of thorns was yours,
that the crown of glory might be mine.
The death was yours,
the life purchased by it mine.
You paid the price,
that I might enjoy the inheritance.

William Penn

King Charles II of England owed William Penn's father, a military hero, a small fortune. The king didn't have the money to pay the family at Admiral Sir William Penn's death, so he offered them forty-five thousand acres of land in the New World. William Penn (1644–1718) called the area Sylvania, the Latin word for woods. Charles added the prefix "Penn" to honor the family, hence the name Pennsylvania.

The king's land grant ignored Native Americans living on the land. The king said, "The indigenous savages have no more right to the land than squirrels and rabbits." William did not share his dim view. He wrote a letter in 1681 to the Lenape tribe, who inhabited Pennsylvania. He explained how the English king had given him a charter to the land, yet he also recognized that the land rightfully belonged to them. He sought their support in settling there and promised to negotiate a fair land purchase with them. He acknowledged injustices that other colonists had perpetrated against them.

I recently read Nathaniel Philbrick's book *Mayflower*. It's not a flattering account of how European settlers treated Native Americans. While there are good-news stories like Squanto and the Thanksgiving feast, there is also a pattern of broken treaties and failed promises. Voltaire once remarked that the treaty between William Penn and the Indians was "the only treaty sworn to and never broken."

William knew his Bible intimately. The Genesis account that all people are created in God's image with inherent dignity and worth left its mark on him. He was a Quaker who followed Jesus in every dimension of life. Consider his prayer for those who grieve the loss of loved ones.

We give back to you, O God, those whom you gave to us.
You did not lose them when you gave them to us,
and we do not lose them by their return to you.
Your dear Son has taught us that life is eternal and love cannot die.
So death is only a horizon, and a horizon is only the limit of our sight.
Open our eyes to see more clearly,
and draw us closer to you,
that we may know that we are nearer to our loved ones who are with you.
You have told us that you are preparing a place for us:
prepare us also for that happy place,
that where you are we may also be always,
O dear Lord of life and death.

François Fénelon

François Fénelon (1651–1715) was way ahead of his time in educating children. After he was ordained a Catholic priest in 1675, he was assigned to teach girls in Paris the essentials of Christian faith. He carefully studied children and the best methods for instructing them. He perfected the art of gentle persuasion instead of using force, which was common in his day. He published a *Treatise on the Education of Girls* that was widely read and highly acclaimed.

After serving as a missionary, François was appointed royal tutor of the duke of Burgundy, the seven-year-old grandson of King Louis XIV and heir to the French throne. His nickname "Little Terror" tells you something about the challenging assignment. François taught his temperamental student by writing him a novel, *The Adventures of Telemachus*, which became the most widely read book in eighteenth-century France after the Bible. The novel highlights the attributes of a wise king through a series of action adventures, functioning as a manual on best practices of leadership. It takes aim at court luxury and greed and warns of expansionist wars. So guess what? The king took offense at the digs on his authoritarian monarchy and banned François from court. François retreated from Versailles to Cambrai, where he continued his writing and served as archbishop. One of his observations about war seems particularly well suited to our time: "All wars are civil wars because all men are brothers."

I find his following prayer instructive about asking God for what we need beyond our limited awareness.

Lord, I know not what I ought to ask of you;
you only know what I need.
You love me more than I know how to love myself.
Father, give to me, your child,
that which I know not how to ask for.
I dare not ask for either crosses or consolations;
I simply present myself before you,
and open my heart to you.
Behold my needs that I know not myself;
see and do according to your tender mercy.
Smite or heal; depress me or raise me up;
I adore all your purposes without knowing them.
I am silent.
I offer myself in sacrifice; I yield myself to you.
I would have no other desire than to accomplish your will.
Teach me to pray.
Pray yourself in me.
Amen.

Susanna Wesley

Susanna and Samuel were married for forty-six years. They did not have an easy time of it. They possessed strong personalities and definite opinions. Case in point: politics. Susanna supported King James II while Samuel preferred his successor, King William. One day at family prayers, Samuel prayed for King William, but Susanna refused to "Amen" his prayer. Samuel regarded her slight as unforgivable and pressed for an apology. Susanna agreed to ask for a pardon if she was proven wrong but would do so only for the sake of expediency. She said to do otherwise would be a lie and therefore a sin. Samuel left the house upset. "You and I must part, for if we have two kings, we must have two beds," he fumed. Samuel was gone six months! They reconciled only after King William died.

Susanna Wesley (1669–1742) was a remarkable woman of faith, and prayer was central to her. Not that everything was smooth sailing. Nine of her and Samuel's nineteen children died in infancy. Their home burned to the ground twice, and Samuel spent time in debtors' prison. Susanna homeschooled their ten children. Her daughters received the same rigorous education as her sons, a practice unheard of in those days. Two sons became influential Christians: John Wesley was a leader of the First Great Awakening in England, an evangelical revival out of which Methodism was birthed, and Charles Wesley became one of the church's great hymn writers.

Susanna's children remember their mom with a towel over her head as a means of finding solitude for prayer. I love her candor and passion in prayer.

Enable me, O God, to collect and compose my thoughts before an immediate approach to you in prayer. May I be careful to have my mind in order when I take upon myself the honor to speak to the sovereign Lord of the universe. . . . You are infinitely too great to be trifled with, too wise to be imposed upon by mock devotion, and I know you abhor a sacrifice without a heart. Help me to entertain a habitual sense of your perfections as an admirable help against cold and formal performances. Save me from engaging in rash and precipitate prayers and from abrupt breaking away to follow business and pleasure as though I had never prayed. Amen.

Isaac Watts

Isaac and his father left church Sunday morning in 1690. Isaac, a teenager at the time, complained to his dad that the singing was dreadfully boring and old-fashioned. "Well then, young man," his father said, "why don't you give us something better to sing?" Isaac took up the challenge. He composed a hymn that week, shared it with the music director of his church, and the congregation sang it the following Sunday in worship. People were enthusiastic about Isaac's new hymn and urged him to write more for them to sing. He generated one hymn each week based on the morning lesson. When word spread, leaders in other area churches protested that these newfangled songs were a decided break from the customary line-by-line singing of the Psalms. Well, what do you know? Complaining about new songs in church is a time-honored tradition!

The writer of these new hymns, Isaac Watts (1674–1748), is known today as the father of English hymnody. He wrote more than seven hundred hymns for use in churches. We have Isaac to thank for "Joy to the World," "Jesus Shall Reign," and "When I Survey the Wondrous Cross," to name but a few. One of my favorites, "O God, Our Help in Ages Past," is a paraphrase of Psalm 90. Although he originally composed it as a nine-verse hymn, most hymnals include only five verses.

Many hymns double as prayers. In the words of Augustine, "Those who sing pray twice."

O God, our help in ages past,
Our hope for years to come,
Our shelter from the stormy blast,
And our eternal home:

Before the hills in order stood,
Or earth received her frame,
From everlasting thou art God,
To endless years the same.

A thousand ages in thy sight
Are like an evening gone,
Short as the watch that ends the night,
Before the rising sun.

Time, like an ever-rolling stream,
Bears all its sons away;
They fly, forgotten, as a dream
Dies at the opening day.

O God, our help in ages past,
Our hope for years to come,
Be thou our guard while life shall last,
And our eternal home.

Gerhard Tersteegen

John of the Cross in the sixteenth century coined the phrase "dark night of the soul" to describe a crisis of faith precipitated by an absence of God. This dark night can be intermittent or prolonged. In the case of Gerhard Tersteegen (1697–1769), it lasted five years.

Gerhard worked as an apprentice for a successful merchant in Germany. He quit his job and moved to the country to seek after God. Initially, it did not go well. He had no real sense of God and became spiritually depressed. Divisions among Christians and the prosperity of evil people distressed him. Feelings of unworthiness led to his self-imposed exile from worship and the Lord's Supper.

One morning, while on a journey to a nearby town and meditating on Scripture, his mood lifted. New appreciation for the redeeming work of Christ punctured a hole in his darkness and nourished him in peace. The transformation was immediate and long-lasting. He became an itinerant preacher. People flocked to his home for spiritual guidance, and he had to move into larger quarters to accommodate the crowds. He wrote poems and hymns expressing his newfound gratitude. One such hymn, "Thou Hidden Love of God," reflects on his five-year bout with spiritual depression. God's absence is not a real absence but a seeming absence, Gerhard came to discover. Even in dark times, God remains faithful.

Another of his prayers leads us to find our rest and strength in God.

O Lord, thy hands have formed us,
and thou hast sent us into this world,
that we may walk in the way that leads to heaven and thyself,
and may find lasting rest in thee
who art the Source and Center of our souls.
Look in pity on us poor pilgrims in the narrow way;
let us not go astray,
but reach at last our true home where our Father dwells.
Guide and govern us from day to day,
and bestow on us food and strength for body and soul,
that we may journey on in peace.
Forgive us for having so often wavered or looked back,
and let us henceforth march straight on in the way of thy laws,
and may our last step be a safe and peaceful passage
to the arms of thy love,
and the blessed fellowship of the saints in light.
Hear us, O Lord, and glorify thy name in us,
that we may glorify thee forever and ever.
Amen.

John Wesley

Imagine yourself sitting in a small gathering of Christians. The appointed leader asks the same questions of each participant. You know the questions beforehand since they are asked at every meeting. How will you answer when the questions are asked of you?

- Am I consciously or unconsciously creating the impression that I am better than I really am?
- In other words, am I a hypocrite?
- Am I honest in all my actions and words, or do I exaggerate?
- Do I confidently pass on to others what was told to me in confidence?

I could go on—there are twenty-two questions in all—but you get the drift.

We would *never* ask such penetrating questions in our time. They would be considered a gross invasion of privacy and possible grounds for legal action. But to John Wesley (1703–1791) and people like him, these questions were intended to help believers grow into fully formed, mature disciples. John first asked them of himself and of five fellow students in a Christian group at Oxford. He led a reform movement in the Church of England that came to be known as Methodism. It was meant as a derogatory term to mock its adherents' fastidious attention to religious methods. (Get it? Method-ists!) It was never John's ambition to break away from the Church of England. His purpose was to restore to it ardor and spiritual passion. He became legendary for his circuit riding (four thousand miles annually on horseback) throughout England and America to support Methodist "societies."

The following prayer by John expresses total surrender and is characteristic of the way he lived his life.

I am no longer my own, but yours.
Put me to what you will, place me with whom you will.
Put me to doing, put me to suffering.
Let me be put to work for you or set aside for you,
Praised for you or criticized for you.
Let me be full, let me be empty.
Let me have all things, let me have nothing.
I freely and fully surrender all things to your glory and service.
And now, O most wonderful and holy God, Creator,
*   Redeemer and Sustainer,*
You are mine and I am yours. So be it.
And the covenant which I have made on earth, let it also be made in heaven.
Amen.

David Brainerd

On the campus of Yale Divinity School is a building called Brainerd Hall. It may be the only building on a college or seminary campus named after an expelled student. David Brainerd (1718–1747) was a third-year student preparing for Christian ministry. Several preachers of the Second Great Awakening visited Yale and made a deep impact on students like David. Tensions escalated among newly awakened students and a less enthusiastic faculty. David was overheard to have said of his tutor that he had "no more grace than a chair." Although David was an exemplary student, he was summarily expelled for his demeaning remark.

Since only graduates from Yale or Harvard were eligible to become ministers in the state of Connecticut, David had to start over. He became a missionary to Native Americans before succumbing to tuberculosis at age twenty-nine. The great Puritan preacher Jonathan Edwards was so impressed by David's devotion that he published *The Diary and Journal of David Brainerd* after his death.

Despite sickness, depression, and physical hardship, David displayed a vital, unquenchable faith. One quote from his diary grabs me: "Lord, let me make a difference for you that is utterly disproportionate to who I am." God answered his prayer big-time. Though he served as a missionary for only four years, he exerted an outsize influence on future generations of pastors and missionaries through his diary. Here is an excerpt.

Blessed Lord!
Let me climb up near to Thee,
and love, and long, and plead, and wrestle with Thee,
and pant for deliverance from the body of sin and death.
Alas! my soul mourns
to think it should ever lose sight of its Beloved again.
O come, Lord Jesus.
Amen.

Samson Occom

I have preached in challenging, supercharged moments, but none can compare with the moment Samson Occom (1723–1792) took the pulpit at Moses Paul's execution. A heated argument after drinking had broken out at David Clark's Tavern in Bethany, Connecticut, one December evening in 1771 between Moses Paul, a Native American, and Moses Cook, a European American, and it turned fatal. Paul admitted to killing Cook (though he claimed it was in self-defense) and was sentenced to hanging, the first Connecticut execution in twenty-three years.

Moses Paul asked Samson Occom, a well-known Mohegan Presbyterian minister, to speak on his execution day. It was customary in those days for a sermon to precede public executions, to transform the spectacle into a moment of moral and spiritual significance. People were eager to hear what "a praying Indian" would say to a dying one, so several thousand gathered at First Congregational Church in New Haven to witness the event.

Samson based his remarks on Romans 6:23: "For the wages of sin is death, but the gift of God is eternal life through Jesus our Lord." He began with the observation that "whether we concern ourselves with death or not, it will concern itself with us." He focused on two principal themes: the universality of human sin and God's gift of salvation through Jesus Christ. In his application, he spoke first to "my poor, unhappy brother Moses." While "your sins have found you out," Samson told him, God's gift of salvation is "good news on this last day of your life." In his remarks to the white establishment, whom he addressed only as "Sirs," he reminded them they were all dying creatures and needed, like Moses, to repent and believe the gospel. To his last constituency, "my kindred in the flesh," he issued a call to temperance. Alcohol was a factor in the murder, which only served to fuel the stereotype of Native Americans as "drunken Indians." He closed with the appeal, "Break off your drunkenness with a gospel repentance and believe in the Lord Jesus Christ." The sermon was widely distributed and reprinted well into the nineteenth century.

There's so much more to the story of Samson Occom, who was sent on a preaching mission to England to raise funds to start a school to train

Native American missionaries. After he had invested three years, preached three hundred sermons, and raised large sums of money, the funds were diverted to start Dartmouth College.

One of Samson's hymns is a prayer of self-consecration upon waking up.

> *Now the shades of night are gone,*
> *Now the morning light is come.*
> *Lord, may we be thine today;*
> *Drive the shades of sin away.*
>
> *Fill our souls with heav'nly light,*
> *Banish doubt and cleanse our sight.*
> *In thy service, Lord, today*
> *Help us labor, help us pray.*
>
> *Keep our haughty passions bound,*
> *Save us from our foes around;*
> *Going out and coming in,*
> *Keep us safe from ev'ry sin.*
>
> *When our work of life is past,*
> *Oh, receive us safe at last!*
> *Night of sin will be no more,*
> *When we reach the heav'nly shore.*

Tikhon of Zadonsk

Nothing is wasted where God is concerned. God can use everything in our lives for redemptive purposes. Tikhon (Timothy) of Zadonsk (1724–1783) was born into extreme poverty in Russia. He spent his childhood doing hard peasant labor for a daily slice of bread.

As a thirteen-year-old, Tikhon was given a state grant to enter seminary and excelled in his studies. He later became a bishop and monk in the Russian Orthodox Church. Though he lived in a monastery, he longed to minister among peasants and common people. He often traveled to neighboring villages to visit the poor and imprisoned. He was once engaged in conversation at a friend's home with a nobleman who didn't believe in God. Tikhon gently refuted the man's atheism. The nobleman suddenly lashed out and struck him in the face. Tikhon responded by falling at the man's feet and begging his forgiveness for having led him to such irritation. Tikhon's humble gesture stunned the nobleman and softened his heart, leading to his conversion. Tikhon said to any who would listen, "Forgiveness is better than revenge." Fyodor Dostoevsky was sufficiently impressed with his character that he modeled the spiritual dynamism of Father Zosima in *The Brothers Karamazov* after Tikhon and his teachings.

Since you came into the world for all, O Savior,
therefore, you came for me, for I am one of all.
You came into the world to save sinners;
therefore, you came to save me also,
for I am one of the sinners.
You came to find and to save those who are lost;
therefore, you came to seek me too,
for I am one of the lost.

O Lord, . . . I should have come to you,
as a transgressor of your law.
I should have fallen at your feet,
cast myself down before you,
humbly begging forgiveness,
pleading with you and craving your mercy.
But you yourself have come to me,
wretched and good-for-nothing servant that I am;
my Lord has come to me. . . .
My Master has come and bestowed his love upon me.

Listen, my soul: God has come to us;
our Lord has visited us. . . .

How shall I repay your generosity? . . .
How shall I thank you? . . .
How shall I repay you? . . .
I shall offer you a grateful heart.

Robert Robinson

Robert Robinson (1735–1790) was riding in a stagecoach. To break the monotony of the trip, a fellow passenger began to hum the hymn "Come, Thou Fount of Every Blessing." The young woman asked Robert what he thought of the song. "Madam, I am the poor, unhappy man who wrote that hymn many years ago, and I would give a thousand worlds, if I had them, if I could feel now as I felt then." Her response is classic: "Sir, the streams of mercy are still flowing," a line taken straight from the hymn.

It's not known whether Robert ever made his way back to God. This widely told story depicts the all-too-common spiritual malady of wandering from God. Robert used to run with a street gang in London. They had planned to heckle the evangelist George Whitefield as he was preaching, but instead his sermon struck a responsive chord in Robert, and he surrendered his life to Christ. He became a Baptist minister, yet he reached a point years later when his own sermons no longer made sense to him, and he became tormented with doubt. His hymn about wandering proved prophetic in his own life.

I identify especially with the last verse. "Prone to wander, Lord, I feel it; prone to leave the God I love." It's a hymn that functions like a prayer. "Let thy goodness, like a fetter, bind my wand'ring heart to thee." My sentiments entirely!

Come, thou fount of every blessing,
Tune my heart to sing thy grace;
Streams of mercy, never ceasing,
Call for songs of loudest praise.
Teach me some melodious sonnet,
Sung by flaming tongues above.
Praise the mount! I'm fixed upon it,
Mount of thy redeeming love.

Here I raise my Ebenezer;
Hither by thy help I'm come.
And I hope, by thy good pleasure,
Safely to arrive at home.
Jesus sought me when a stranger,
Wand'ring from the fold of God.
He, to rescue me from danger,
Interposed his precious blood.

O to grace how great a debtor
Daily I'm constrained to be!
Let thy goodness, like a fetter,
Bind my wand'ring heart to thee.
Prone to wander, Lord, I feel it;
Prone to leave the God I love.
Here's my heart; O take and seal it,
Seal it for thy courts above.

Richard Allen

Stokely Sturgis was an eighteenth-century Delaware farmer and enslaver. One of the people he enslaved was named Richard (1760–1831). Three of Richard's five siblings along with his mother had been previously sold to a plantation far away from him.

Richard had a dramatic conversion to Christ at age seventeen while attending a Methodist gathering in the woods. Stokely took notice of his genuine faith, so much so that he started asking probing questions about it. Richard told him, "Sir, I would ask Rev. Garretson to come and preach right here to your house. He can answer your questions much better than I can." Stokely took Richard's suggestion. When Freeborn Garretson (what a name!), a white abolitionist, preached at his home, Stokely heard the gospel and became a Christian. He fell under the conviction that enslaving people was wrong. Because he was in serious debt, he was unwilling to release Richard on the spot, but he worked out a deal for Richard to buy his freedom for two thousand dollars. After work hours, Richard drove a wagon delivering salt and preaching the gospel wherever he went.

Three years later, in 1780, Richard bought his freedom and changed his name to Richard Allen. He purchased a blacksmith shop, which he converted into a church, and in 1794 founded a new denomination, the African Methodist Episcopal Church, so that Black people could worship God without racial oppression. Richard, who had taught himself to read and write, also opened schools for Black children, and he and his wife, Sarah, ran a station for the Underground Railroad. What God can do with people who take God at his word!

We believe, O God, that you have not abandoned us to the dim light of our own reason to conduct us to happiness, but that you have revealed in Holy Scripture whatever is necessary for us to believe and practice. How noble and exalted are the precepts, how sublime and enlightening the truth, how persuasive and strong the motives, how powerful the assistance of your holy religion. Our delight shall be in your statutes, and we will not forget your Word. Amen.

Charlotte Elliott

Charlotte Elliott (1789–1871) led a comfortable life with her family in Clapham, England. She was carefree and lighthearted. Her days were occupied with drawing people's portraits and writing funny poems. It all came crashing down when she became seriously ill shortly after her thirtieth birthday. She spent the balance of her life dealing with chronic pain and fatigue. In the language of the Victorian era, she was an "invalid."

In 1834, Charlotte went to live with her brother Henry, a Church of England pastor who was leading a campaign to raise money to build a school for daughters of poor clergy. Members of Henry's church were busy on the eve of a big fundraising bazaar—minus Charlotte, who stayed behind. She went to bed that evening feeling useless. Her discouragement didn't stop there. By the middle of the night, she was questioning her existence and sinking deeper into despondency.

On the day of the bazaar, with thoughts from the previous evening pressing down on her, she pulled herself together to compose "the grand certainties of her faith." When she wrote, "I am accepted in the Beloved, just as I am," the words began to flow. A poem quickly took shape, which she shared with her sister-in-law. It was later set to music, and "Just as I Am" became Billy Graham's signature hymn during his crusades.

Reflecting on his sister's hymn, Henry wrote, "In the course of a long ministry I hope I have been permitted to see some fruit of my labor, but I find more has been done by a simple hymn of my sister's." When the hymn was first published, it was accompanied by Jesus's words "Whoever comes to me I will never cast out" (John 6:37). Four stanzas are reproduced here, inviting us to come to Jesus just as we are.

Just as I am, without one plea,
But that thy blood was shed for me,
And that thou bidst me come to thee,
O Lamb of God, I come! I come!

Just as I am, though tossed about
With many a conflict, many a doubt,
Fightings within, and fears without,
O Lamb of God, I come, I come!

Just as I am, thou wilt receive,
Wilt welcome, pardon, cleanse, relieve,
Because thy promise I believe;
O Lamb of God, I come, I come!

Just as I am, thy love unknown
Has broken every barrier down;
Now to be thine, yea, thine alone,
O Lamb of God, I come, I come!

Thomas Arnold

Character development has all but disappeared from American education. In the rush to achieve higher test scores, schools have left character education off the curriculum. Value-free education will become a house of cards. Character education and academic achievement work in tandem.

Thomas Arnold (1795–1842) was an English educator who believed character formation should be a primary aim of school curricula. Rugby School in England was regarded as one of the worst schools when he became headmaster in 1828. Bullying, cheating, theft, and sexual impropriety were rampant among its students. Thomas took over as chaplain to preach powerful and moving sermons to students. He instituted a practice whereby students could meet with him privately, which was unheard of at the time. He trained faculty to devote as much time to moral character as they did to academic rigor. In the words of one former student, Thomas "seemed to have the freshest view of the Lord's life and death that I ever knew a man to possess." Under his leadership, Rugby School became a model of public-school reform in England and famous for its successful graduates.

Some educators in our day insist values are the exclusive domain of the home, not public schools. Baloney! Let's recover Thomas Arnold's focus on character formation to complement intellectual development. This featured prayer from Thomas was offered in a chapel service at Rugby School in 1841.

O Lord, . . . give thy blessing to our daily work,
that we may do it in faith and heartily,
as to the Lord and not for human masters.
All our powers of body and mind are thine,
and we devote them to thy service.
Sanctify them and the work in which they are engaged.
Let us not be slothful but fervent in spirit.
O Lord, so bless our efforts
that they may bring forth in us the fruits of true wisdom. . . .
Save us from all pride, vanity, and reliance on our power.
Teach us to seek truth and enable us to gain it,
but grant that we may ever speak the truth in love,
that while we know earthly things,
we may know thee, and be known by thee,
in and through thy Son Jesus Christ.
Give us this day thy Holy Spirit
that we may be yours in body and spirit
in all our work and all our refreshments
through Jesus Christ thy Son, our Lord.
Amen.

Sojourner Truth

She resolved to escape her enslaver to gain freedom. She had been bought and sold so many times by and to cruel men that she was ready to do whatever it took to leave it all behind. Isabella Baumfree (ca. 1797–1883) told God she was afraid to flee at night, yet during the day everyone would see her. A thought flashed into her mind: go at dawn. "Thank you, God, for the thought," she prayed, and with the morning light, she left with her infant daughter, Sophia, and all her belongings in a sack.

She asked God for asylum. She had been told that Quakers might assist in her rescue—they were people who lived strictly by Jesus's teachings. She knocked reluctantly at the home of a Quaker family. Isaac and Maria Van Wagenen opened their heart and home to her. When her enslaver demanded her return, Isaac said they didn't believe in slavery, yet he purchased her services for the balance of the year for twenty-five dollars. When Isabella tried to address Isaac as her new master, he corrected her, the first time a white man had ever refused the title. He told her, "There is one master, and he who is your master is mine also." Isabella learned the way of Jesus in the Van Wagenen home. They helped her win back freedom for her young son, Peter.

Isabella became an itinerant preacher and plain-speaking abolitionist, changing her name to Sojourner Truth. She is best known for her "Ain't I a Woman?" speech at an 1851 women's rights convention in Akron, Ohio. Her take on women's rights makes me smile: "Where did Christ come from? From God and woman. Men had nothing to do with him." Her travels took her to the White House to visit Abraham Lincoln. Proceeds from her book, *The Narrative of Sojourner Truth*, which she dictated (she never learned to read or write), made it possible for her to purchase a home and retire comfortably. There is a sculpture in her honor, the first for a Black woman, in the US Capitol.

Her conversational manner is evident in the following prayer for the release of her son Peter from slavery.

Oh God, you know how much I am distressed, for I have told you again and again. Now, God, help me get my son. If you were in trouble, as I am, and I could help you, as you can me, think I wouldn't do it? Yes, God, you know I would do it. Oh God, you know I have no money, but you can make the people do for me, and you must make the people do for me. I will never give you peace till you do, God. Oh God, make the people hear me—don't let them turn me off without hearing and helping me.

Albert Barnes

The struggle between the old guard and new guard is nothing new. The old guard wants to preserve the past and maintain the status quo, while the new guard seeks alternative ways to usher in the future. Presbyterians in the early nineteenth century were locked in a colossal tug-of-war between old and new guard. The old guard, calling themselves Old School Presbyterians, held to a strict interpretation of the Westminster Confession of Faith from the early 1600s. A younger generation of Presbyterians, labeled the New School, supported the innovative revival strategies of evangelists like Charles Finney to promote the gospel on the American frontier. Old School Presbyterians accused Finney of trying to manipulate people into decisions for Christ instead of waiting on the Holy Spirit to do his genuine work.

Albert Barnes (1798–1870) was a young, earnest minister caught in the crossfire. He was put forward as the new pastoral candidate for First Presbyterian Church in Philadelphia in 1835. The Old School Presbyterians took issue with Albert's commentary on Romans and the mere suggestion that people could exercise their wills in accepting or denying Christ. They accused him of doctrinal heresy and brought him to trial in the Philadelphia presbytery. The trial dragged on for four days.

Albert's demeanor during the investigation was exemplary. This was a man who wouldn't fish with a hook because he considered it a form of deception and a violation of Jesus's teaching in Matthew 17:27. Ultimately, he was acquitted, yet some detractors were unsatisfied and brought a second unsuccessful heresy charge a year later.

What did Albert do to occupy his time during his trials? He composed *A Manual of Prayer* on every conceivable topic from accountability to zeal. Given his heresy trial, his prayer offered here is most exceptional.

Lord, preserve me from falsehood. Teach me that it degrades character, injures peace of conscience, subverts the welfare of society, and incurs thy hot displeasure. O make my conscience tender with regard to every violation of truth. Let me not utter falsehood in jest; for thou hast said that for every idle word we shall speak, we shall give account on the day of judgment. Let me not depart from truth for the love of gain, for the wages of sin is death. Let me not practice deceit through the fear or favor of man, for his breath is in his nostrils. And, O Lord, let me not be false, with the plea of doing good, for we may not do evil that good may come. Keep me, I pray thee, from everything which is prejudicial to truth, or injurious to my own or my neighbor's good name. Suffer me not to think, nor act, nor speak deceitfully in anything.

O Lord, make me, above all, sincere toward thee. Let me not attempt to draw nigh to thee with lip service, while my heart is far from thee. . . . May all my homage before thee spring from a controlling desire to do thy will, which requires truth in the inward parts.

Titus Coan

A large company of friends gathered at Boston Harbor on a blustery day in December 1834 to bid a tearful farewell to Titus Coan (1801–1882) and his wife, Fidelia. They knelt for prayer and sang a final hymn together. The couple boarded the merchant ship *Hellespont* and set sail for the Sandwich Islands (now Hawaii). They arrived six months later after a perilous journey to begin their missionary endeavors.

Titus centered ministry in the small city of Hilo on the Big Island. Having learned the Hawaiian language in three months, he set off on a foot tour. He resolved to meet all sixteen thousand people who lived on the island. He climbed volcanic mountains, forged raging streams, crossed dangerous ravines, and endured drenching rains. Yet he wrote in his journal, "I would not exchange my humble toil among them [the people of the Sandwich Islands] for the throne of England." He kept careful notes of everyone he met, recording their responses to the gospel and following up a year later to assess their progress. He also kept copious notes of active volcanoes.

Titus, who came to faith during the Second Great Awakening, was now witnessing a revival that would last six years. One evening in Hilo at a prayer service, when he was preaching on the prophet Isaiah's words "Prepare the way of the Lord," a tidal wave swept away one hundred homes and thirteen people drowned. Coming so close to death, people realized their great need for God and turned to Christ. One Sunday in 1839, Titus took a bucket of water and baptized 1,705 new believers. By the time he left the island in 1870 for a speaking tour of the US, sixty self-supporting churches had been planted.

In July 1831, during his student days at Auburn Theological Seminary, Titus wrote the following prayer.

Lord, send me where thou wilt,
only go with me;
lay on me what thou wilt,
only sustain me;
cut every cord
but the one which binds me
to thy cause, to thy heart.

Anthony Ashley-Cooper, 7th Earl of Shaftesbury

You won't find her name enshrined among the great saints in the church, but Maria Mills certainly belongs in the spiritual hall of fame. She was housekeeper for the 6th Earl of Shaftesbury and his wife, Lady Spencer. Anthony Ashley-Cooper (1801–1885) was their eldest son, born into wealth and privilege—yet it was a loveless home. His dad was a tyrant, and Anthony wrote about his mother's "dereliction of duty and harshness."

Enter Maria Mills, who supplied what Anthony's parents lacked. She introduced Anthony to prayer and taught him the stories of Jesus. One of Anthony's biographers wrote that Maria "spoke of the Lord Jesus as the risen Redeemer who could be a friend."

Her influence was long-lasting. Anthony became the 7th Earl of Shaftesbury, a member of Parliament, and a tireless social reformer. As he witnessed the plight of the poor, he wrote, "I must persist, . . . but it is a formidable step. God alone can strengthen me." He pressed for more humane laws to regulate young children working in factories and coal mines. He advocated for better housing for the poor and the reform of "lunatic asylums" (the name itself tells you something about the typical nineteenth-century approach to mental illness).

Anthony's achievements in Parliament were nothing short of stunning. He wrote, "My religious views are not very popular, but they are views that have sustained and comforted me all through my life. If a man's religion is worth anything, it should enter into every sphere of life and rule his conduct in every relation."

O God, the Father of the forsaken, the help of the weak, the supplier of the needy, you teach us that love toward the human race is the bond of perfectness and the imitation of your blessed self. Open and touch our hearts that we may see and do, both for this world and for that which is to come, the things that belong to our peace. Strengthen us in the work which we have undertaken; give us wisdom, perseverance, faith, and zeal; and in your own time and according to your pleasure, prosper the issues, for the love of your Son, Jesus Christ. Amen.

John Henry Newman

When I was new to pastoral ministry and asked to conduct graveside services, I relied on a book of suggested prayers for use at funerals. I was drawn to the prayer that follows here, for it seems a fitting way to conclude a burial. Years later, I learned it is the contribution of an Anglican turned Roman Catholic priest named John Henry Newman (1801–1890). He attended an Anglican church with his family as a child and learned the catechism, but his was merely a formal adherence to Christianity. He said of that time, "I formed no religious convictions until I was fifteen."

When he left home for boarding school, a great change came over him. As an avid reader, he became engrossed in the story of Augustine's conversion recounted in his *Confessions*. An Anglican priest at Pembroke School served as "the human means of this beginning of divine faith in me." His trust in God became, in his own words, "more certain than I have hands and feet."

John sent shock waves through the Church of England when he joined the Roman Catholic Church in middle age and became a priest. His decision delighted Catholics, upset his family, and added fuel to the Protestant-Catholic divide. Many wrote that he "converted" to Catholicism. Converted? Every time I encounter this word in Scripture, it is used in relation to Jesus. We join churches; we convert to Jesus. I like what one of John's Anglican colleagues, Edward Pusey, said about John's decision to switch churches: he described it as being "transplanted to another part of the vineyard."

We close with his prayer that trusts God's mercy in life and death.

O Lord, support us all the day long,
till the shadows lengthen,
and the evening comes,
and the busy world is hushed,
and the fever of life is over,
and our work is done.
Then, in thy mercy, give us a safe lodging,
a holy rest, and peace at the last,
through Jesus Christ our Lord.
Amen.

Phoebe Palmer

Tragedy leads people toward God or away from God. For Phoebe Palmer (1807–1874), personal crisis became an impetus for closer union with God. Phoebe was raised in Methodist revivalism when conversion was regarded as a highly emotional experience. It never happened to Phoebe this way. Her conversion was more subdued and gradual. She married Walter, a fellow believer, who sensed God's call to become a doctor.

Crisis struck early in their home. Their oldest child, Alexander, died at nine months, and a second son, Samuel, died at seven weeks. Phoebe was convinced God was punishing her lack of faith. The bottom fell out of their lives when their eleven-month-old daughter Eliza died in a fire accidentally set by a maid.

That was it. Phoebe decided "to lay it all on the altar" and offer herself completely to God. She stopped blaming herself and others for the tragedy and resolved to devote the time she would have given Eliza to the Lord's work.

Phoebe became a dominant force in the nineteenth-century Holiness movement. She organized with her sister a weekly Tuesday prayer meeting for the "promotion of holiness" in her home, which had to be enlarged to handle the crowd. She and Walter became itinerant evangelists during a time when women took heat for doing so. They started the Five Points Mission in an impoverished neighborhood in New York City, which has served as a model for modern urban ministry.

At age eleven, Phoebe wrote a poem on the flyleaf of her Bible that closed with the words "Henceforth, I take thee as my future guide. Let not from thee my youthful heart divide. And then, if late or early death be mine, all will be well, since I, O Lord, am thine." At eleven, I was still putting baseball cards in the spokes of my bike to make it sound like a motorcycle.

In 1845, after her daughter Eliza's death, Phoebe wrote a covenant to God that solidified her resolve to give her entire self to God.

In the name and in the presence of the triune Deity, Father, Son, and Holy Ghost, I do hereby consecrate body, soul, and spirit, time, talents, influence, family, and estate—all with which I stand connected, near or remote, to be forever, and in the most unlimited sense, THE LORD'S.

My body I lay upon thine altar, O Lord, that it may be a temple for the Holy Spirit to dwell in. From henceforth I rely upon thy promise, that thou wilt live and walk in me, believing, as I now surrender myself for all coming time to thee, that thou dost condescend to enter this thy temple, and dost from this solemn moment hallow it with thy indwelling presence. . . .

Confessing that I am utterly unable to keep one of the least of thy commandments, unless endued with power from on high, I hereby covenant to trust in thee for the needful aid of thy Spirit. Thou dost now behold my entire being presented to thee a living sacrifice. . . .

O Christ, thou dost accept the sacrifice, and through thy meritorious life and death, the infinite efficacy of the blood of the everlasting covenant, thou dost accept me as thine forever. . . .

And now, O Lord, I will hold fast the profession of this my faith. . . . And as I solemnly purpose that I would sooner die than break my covenant engagements with thee, so will I, in obedience to the command of God, hold fast the profession of my faith unwaveringly, in the face of an accusing enemy and an accusing world. And this I will through thy grace do, irrespective of my emotions. Amen.

Wilhelm Loehe

The life of Wilhelm Loehe (1808–1872) represents the triumph of faith over circumstances. After completing his theological studies at the University of Erlangen, he expected to receive an appointment to a city church. Instead, he was assigned to pastor a small church in an obscure farming village called Neuendettelsau (it even sounds out-of-the-way), a place where he initially said he would not want his dog buried.

He stayed thirty-six years! His wife died at twenty-four, leaving him to raise four young children alone. He was concerned about the under-privileged status of single women and widows in his community, so he established a center to serve as the headquarters for women's social and educational activities.

He read an account of the spiritual needs of German Lutherans on the American frontier and the plight of Native Americans. His conscience would not let him rest until he did something to meet the need. He organized a training institute to prepare pastors for mission service in the American Midwest and founded two schools in the States (now Wartburg College and Concordia Seminary). He sent missionaries to Brazil, New Guinea, Australia, and Ukraine. On his tombstone are etched the words "I believe in the communion of the saints."

From an unlikely place, Wilhelm brought much-needed renewal to the local church and mission to the wider world.

Ever blessed Trinity,
to your mercy I commit this day
my body and soul,
together with all my ways and undertakings.
Be gracious to me;
enlarge my heart and open my lips,
that I may praise and magnify your name,
which alone is holy.
And as you have made me
for the praise of your holy name,
grant that I may yield my life
in service to your honor,
in humble love and fear.
Amen.

Henry Edward Manning

Working the docks at the port of London was a dangerous job with no benefits and lousy pay. But if you are poor and have no other options, you take what you can get. Every day at the docks, a surging crowd of desperate men showed up, scrambling to be chosen for a few hours to unload cargo ships. When, on August 14, 1889, dock owners announced another wage reduction, workers walked off the job. By the end of the month, one hundred thousand dock workers were out on strike. By early September, the strike had reached crisis stage. Dock workers and their families were now starving to death.

The desperate workers turned to a local priest, Henry Edward Manning (1808–1892), who had previously advocated for the rights of workers. Father Manning was seen as fair and impartial. He put forward a settlement that satisfied both parties and averted a catastrophe. Negotiating a labor agreement isn't work we typically associate with a priest, yet it was the catalyst that brought many to Christ. Later, several leaders in twentieth-century England credited Henry with introducing them to real gospel living.

Henry began his ministry in the Church of England. His first clerical assignment was assisting an Anglican priest who had become ill. When the ailing priest died, Henry served in his place for seventeen years and married his predecessor's daughter. Their marriage, however, was short-lived, as she died four years later. In midcareer he became a Catholic priest and eventually an archbishop and cardinal. Not your typical priest's trajectory!

O Holy Spirit of God,
take me as your disciple.
Guide me,
illumine me,
sanctify me.
Bind my hands,
that they may do no evil;
cover my eyes,
that they may see it no more;
sanctify my heart,
that evil may not dwell within me.
Be my God,
be my guide.
Wherever you lead me,
I will go;
whatever you forbid me,
I will renounce;
whatever you command me,
in your strength, I will do.
Lead me, then,
into the fullness of your truth.
Amen.

Thomas Theullosson Carter

Thomas Theullosson (T. T.) Carter (1808–1901) was twenty-four when he was called to his first pastorate at a small church in rural England. It was a long-standing custom in the church for the rector to give a mince pie, a loaf of bread, and a quart of ale to every man, woman, and child in the parish. Thomas thought it was "an undesirable waste of money." He eliminated the practice and redirected the money to clothes for the poor. He wrote, "I believe reasonable people thought it was the right thing to do. But some, I am afraid, never forgave me." A short while later, he received a parcel on Christmas Day. At the bottom of the package, under a heap of rags and straw, was a mince pie.

It should come as no surprise that Thomas didn't stay long. He went to another church and noted in a letter that the sanctuary was in a state of disrepair. And, he added, "the behavior of the congregation was on a par with the appearance of the sanctuary." To curb drunkenness, he founded a temperance society. He started a relief ministry for the poor and opened a House of Mercy for "fallen women," establishing an Anglican sisterhood to meet the needs of the House of Mercy community. Thomas also reintroduced confession to aid in the renewal effort. Some Anglican colleagues took umbrage at his "ritual excesses," which led to his resignation from the church. He devoted the remainder of his life to the House of Mercy, providing spiritual direction and becoming a pioneer of retreats in England.

Thomas aspired to lead a life of humility. "Humility is the perpetual quietness of heart," he wrote. "It is never to be fretted, or vexed, or irritated, or sore, or disappointed. It is to expect nothing, to wonder at nothing that is done to me, to feel nothing done against me. It is to be at rest when nobody praises me, and when I am blamed and despised."

Near the end of his life, he compiled a book of prayers, titled *Treasury of Devotion*, which includes this Advent prayer.

O Lord Jesus Christ, who for our sake didst vouchsafe to descend from thy throne of glory and from the bosom of the Father to this vale of tears and woe; who wast conceived by the Holy Ghost, born of the Virgin Mary, and was made man: Make, we beseech thee, our hearts a fit habitation for thyself. Beautify and fill them with all spiritual graces, and possess them wholly by thy power. Give us grace to prepare for thy coming with deep humility, to receive thee with burning love, and to hold thee fast with a firm faith, that we may never depart from thee forever. Through thy merits, amen.

Harriet Beecher Stowe

Upon meeting the diminutive writer Harriet Beecher Stowe (1811–1896) in 1862, President Lincoln reportedly said, "So, you are the little woman who started the big war!" Her landmark social novel, *Uncle Tom's Cabin*, might not have caused the Civil War, but it contributed significantly to the slavery debate.

Harriet's father, Lyman Beecher, was an influential Puritan preacher, left to raise eight children when Harriet's mom died when she was five. Harriet came to faith at age thirteen in response to one of her father's sermons. Lyman moved the family to Cincinnati when he became president of Lane Seminary. Harriet was impacted by listening to seminary debates over slavery and witnessing dehumanizing slave auctions along the Ohio River. The death of one of Harriet's sons gave her empathy for the pain enslaved mothers felt when their children were sold and separated from them. Harriet said of her writing, "My vocation is to preach on paper." She originally published *Uncle Tom's Cabin* in weekly installments for an antislavery journal. When it was compiled in book form, it sold three hundred thousand copies in the first year alone. When opponents dismissed her work as fictional, she published documents and testimonials in a sequel, *A Key to Uncle Tom's Cabin*, to validate her story.

Harriet wrote of prayer, "Prayer is a long rope with a strong hold." An early riser, she used to go on walks at 4:30 in the morning "to ponder the things of God." She wrote the hymn "Still, Still with Thee" in 1853, reflecting on her experience of praying at the break of dawn. The hymn opens and closes with the assurance "I am with Thee."

Still, still with Thee—when purple morning breaketh,
When the bird waketh, and the shadows flee;
Fairer than morning, lovelier than the daylight,
Dawns the sweet consciousness, I am with Thee!

Alone with Thee—amid the mystic shadows,
The solemn hush of nature newly born;
Alone with Thee in breathless adoration,
In the calm dew and freshness of the morn.

. . . .

Still, still with Thee! as to each newborn morning
A fresh and solemn splendor still is given,
So doth this blessed consciousness awaking
Breathe, each day, nearness unto Thee and heaven.

When sinks the soul, subdued by toil, to slumber,
Its closing eye looks up to Thee in prayer;
Sweet the repose beneath Thy wings o'ershading,
But sweeter still, to wake and find Thee there.

So shall it be at last, in that bright morning,
When the soul waketh, and life's shadows flee;
Oh! in that hour, fairer than daylight dawning,
Shall rise the glorious thought—I am with Thee.

Anne Brontë

"The Brontë Sisters" sounds like a singing group. They were first-rate novelists in nineteenth-century England. During the Victorian era, it was considered unladylike to be a writer. That's why these three sisters, Charlotte, Emily, and Anne, acquired male-sounding pen names: Currer, Ellis, and Acton Bell. When their mom died young, an aunt came to live with them and teach them about running a household, but they were far more interested in writing poems and short stories.

Anne Brontë (1820–1849) was distinctive in her writing style, more of a realist than the customary Romantic writers of her day. She defended the honest portrayal of her characters: "I would rather depict them as they really are than as they would wish to appear." Anne worked as a governess for two bratty, pampered children. While it was a thankless job, it provided her with plenty of writing material. Her first book, *Agnes Grey*, skewers her culture's obsession with status and class.

Anne's dad, a pastor, was earnest to share the gospel with his daughters, but it was a Moravian pastor who brought the message home to Anne. He visited when she became ill while working as a governess. He wrote of their visits, "I found her well acquainted with the truths of Scripture, but more as law than gospel, more as a requirement for God than the gift of his Son." He concluded, "Her heart opened to the truths of the Bible."

Anne's writing evidences both deep faith and honest doubt. Her poem "Confidence" expresses her ongoing struggles with sin and doubt, yet in the end she falls back on God's love and mercy, as the final two stanzas, reproduced on the next page, show.

Anne died of tuberculosis at age twenty-nine. Her prayer that follows here is the epitome of trust.

I need not fear my foes,
I need not yield to care;
I need not sink beneath my woes,
For thou wilt answer prayer.

In my Redeemer's name,
I give myself to thee,
And all unworthy as I am,
My God will cherish me.

Anna Waring

Poetry makes up a substantial portion of the Bible. Half of the Old Testament was written in poetic form. While English poetry relies on rhyme and meter, Hebrew poetry is far more subtle. It works off imaginative wordplay and makes elaborate use of parallelism, a form of repetition. Reading Hebrew poetry, even in translation, requires an active imagination. Maybe that's why people don't expend the energy to read it. Anna Laetitia Waring (1823–1910) became interested in biblical poetry as a child. She taught herself ancient Hebrew so that she could read Old Testament poetry in its original language. Who does that?

Anna was born in the small Welsh town of Neath and moved to Bristol as a teen, where she lived until her death. She was modest and reluctant to draw attention to her writing, simply signing her poems with the acronym "ALW." Her friends prevailed on her to publish a collection of her poems, which she titled *Hymns and Meditations*, in 1850. It is thought that she suffered from some form of chronic illness. While she makes no pointed reference to it, there are hints in her poetry. For example, wondering at God's role as Comforter, she wrote, "Who would not suffer pain like mine, to be consoled like me?" She could also be lighthearted, as in her whimsical reflections on cats. She was a regular visitor to the local jail. Fellow poets belittled her for investing time in rehabilitating hardened criminals, but she persisted.

One of her poems written in prayer form, "Go Not Far from Me, O My God," is excerpted here. Like many of her poems, it was later sung as a hymn.

Go not far from me, O my God,
Whom all my times obey.
Take from me anything thou wilt,
But go not thou away,
And let the storm that does thy work
Deal with me as it may.

On thy compassion I repose,
In weakness and distress:
I will not ask for greater ease,
Lest I should love thee less.
Oh, 'tis a blessed thing for me
To need thy tenderness.

. . . .

When I am feeble as a child,
And flesh and heart give way,
Then on thy everlasting strength
With passive trust I stay.
And the rough wind becomes a song,
The darkness shines as day.

. . . .

Deep unto deep may call; but I
With peaceful heart will say,
Thy loving-kindness hath a charge
No waves can take away:
And let the storm that speeds me home
Deal with me as it may.

Lucy Larcom

She was a "mill girl," one of the many who worked in the textile factories of Lowell, Massachusetts, in the early nineteenth century. Lucy Larcom (1824–1893) was born into a family of ten children. Her dad, a retired sea captain, taught his children in the way of Jesus until his death in 1832, when Lucy was eight. Her mom, with no income to support ten children, moved to Lowell to become a boarding house manager, cooking and keeping house for forty female workers employed at the mills.

Lucy began working at the mill at age eleven. She worked in the spinning room from 5:00 a.m. to 7:00 p.m., with a half hour for breakfast and lunch. Her weekly pay after room and board was a dollar. She spent ten years working in the mills.

To mitigate the numbing influence of tedious factory work, she turned to poetry. She joined an evening writing group at church and published her poems in a literary magazine, which caught the admiration of fellow poet John Greenleaf Whittier. Her can-do attitude is expressed in her words: "I defied the machinery to make me its slave. Its incessant discord could not drown the music of my thoughts if I would let them fly high enough."

At twenty-two, Lucy moved with her married sister and family to rural Illinois, where she taught in a log cabin schoolhouse. She eventually returned to Lowell to teach at Wheaton Seminary (now Wheaton College in Massachusetts). She continued to write poems that eventually filled fifteen volumes. Her most enduring work is a book of reflections on her growing-up years, *A New England Girlhood*, which provides details on what childhood was like in her day.

Her poetry expresses a deep love of God and trust in Jesus. She wrote, "Whatever science and philosophy may do for mankind, the world can never outgrow its need for the simplicity that is in Christ." The following poem of hers is called "Our Prayers."

Art thou not weary of our selfish prayers?
Forever crying, "Help me, save me, Lord!"
We stay fenced in by petty fears and cares,
Nor hear the song outside, nor join its vast accord.

And yet the truest praying is a psalm:
The lips that open in pure air to sing
Make entrance to the heart for health and balm;
And so life's urn is filled at heaven's all-brimming spring.

Still are we saying, "Teach us how to pray"?
O teach us how to love! and then our prayer
Through other lives will find its upward way,
As plants together seek and find sweet life and air.

Thy large bestowing makes us ask for more:
Prayer widens with the world wherethrough love flows.
Needy, though blest, we throng before thy door:
Let in thy sunshine, Lord, on all that lives and grows!

George MacDonald

George MacDonald's (1824–1905) initial foray into preaching was short-lived. His congregation complained that his preaching was overly imaginative and not dogmatic enough—so much so that he resigned after three years and took up writing, specializing in fantasy literature and children's stories. We have George to thank for influencing C. S. Lewis to explore a life of faith. He remarked after reading George's fantasy novel *Phantastes* that he knew he had "crossed the great frontier" in his evolution from atheism to belief.

In 1880, George wrote a book of 366 poems for use in daily meditation and prayer, which he titled *The Book of Strife in the Form of the Diary of an Old Soul*. Each poem is composed of seven lines with three sets of end rhyme and a solitary punchline at the end. He intended for each poem to appear facing a blank left-hand page for readers to add their personal reflections and prayers.

While it takes time to adjust to George's Scottish style, his deep spirituality and prayerful insights are worth the effort. *Diary of an Old Soul* is an intimate look into his longings, joys, and struggles in everyday life. He was no stranger to hardship. His mother and two of his brothers died during his childhood. He experienced chronic emphysema and periodic bouts of depression. Four of his children preceded him in death. Yet he remained remarkably upbeat and resilient about faith. The following prayer is his entry for January 10.

When I no more can stir my soul to move,
And life is but the ashes of a fire;
When I can but remember that my heart
Once used to live and love, long and aspire,—
Oh, be thou then the first, the one thou art;
Be thou the calling, before all answering love,
And in me wake hope, fear, boundless desire.

Anna Warner

They were known as "Miss Warner's boys." A group of West Point cadets would row their boats across the Hudson River each Sunday afternoon to Constitution Island, where Susan and Anna Warner (1827–1915) lived. Each cadet came with a Bible verse to share, and Susan would lead them in a Bible study. Afterward, sister Anna appeared with fresh lemonade and homemade gingerbread. When Susan died, Anna kept the class going until her death in 1915. Despite repeated efforts by developers to buy the island, Anna willed it to West Point, and the Warner home stands today in the sisters' honor. Susan and Anna are the only two civilians buried at West Point Cemetery.

These two sisters who never married supported themselves with their writing. Susan wrote the novel *Say and Seal* in 1860, a story about Johnny Fax, a critically ill boy who is comforted by John Lindell, his Sunday school teacher. John carries Johnny in his arms as his fever spikes. Johnny begs his teacher to comfort him with singing, so John breaks out into song: "Jesus loves me—this I know, for the Bible tells me so. Little ones to him belong; they are weak, but he is strong." This poetic text was composed by Anna for inclusion in Susan's novel.

It's sobering to think that this popular children's hymn was first written to comfort a dying child. That explains Anna's original words in the last stanza, "Jesus loves me—he will stay close beside me all the way. When at last I come to die, take me home with thee on high." The hymn writer William Bradbury altered the words in 1862 to suit a wider audience and added a chorus, and the song is still sung by believers today, young and old alike.

Another of Anna's poems leads us into prayer.

Jesus, help conquer!
My spirit is sinking,
Deep waters of sorrow go over my head.
Weeping and trembling,
And fearing and shrinking,
I watch for the day and night cometh instead.
Bitter the cup
I am hourly drinking—
How thorny the path that I hourly tread!

. . . .

Jesus, help conquer!
I cry unto thee!
Hardly my heart its petitions can frame:
All is so dark
And so painful to me,
All I can utter, sometimes, is thy name.
Jesus, help conquer!
My portion now be;
Though all else should change, be thou ever the same.

Andrew Murray

My initial thought in writing about Andrew Murray (1828–1917) was to ac-knowledge that I do not belong in his league. He was a spiritual giant. Yet when I read the story of Andrew's marital engagement, I relax. This is more like it, someone with whom I can identify.

Andrew at age twenty-seven was already a capable, confident minister. "Never fear" was his motto. He was sent by the British government to South Africa on a diplomatic assignment and stayed with the Rutherford family in their home. Andrew was attracted to twenty-year-old Emma Rutherford, and he proposed to her prior to his departure. His approach was business-like and his offer poorly timed. Emma was in the middle of helping with a child's birthday party. She was stunned and rendered speechless by the proposal since they had known each other for less than a month. She wrote the next day, flatly refusing his offer. She expressed in a letter to her sister, "It pains me that one of no ordinary mental capacity and vigor of piety should be so totally devoid of proper feelings." Andrew sent an apology to Emma and left the door open to further contact.

After a flurry of letters, Emma reversed course and accepted his mar-riage proposal, with the proviso that they would spend more time together. They were married in 1865 and flourished as a couple for forty-eight years. Andrew credited his blunders with jump-starting his deeper walk with Christ. He served as a South African pastor and a prodigious author. This prayer is taken from his book *With Christ in the School of Prayer*.

O Lord Jesus, teach me to understand and believe what you have promised me. It is not hidden from you, O my Lord, with what reasonings my heart seeks to satisfy itself, when no answer comes. There is the thought that my prayer is not in harmony with the Father's secret counsel; that there is perhaps something better you would give me; or that prayer as fellowship with God is blessing enough without an answer. . . . You did say so plainly that prayer may and must expect an answer. You assure us that this is the fellowship of a child with the Father: the child asks and the Father gives.

Blessed Lord, your words are faithful and true. It must be because I pray amiss that my experience of prayer is not clearer. It must be because I live too little in the Spirit. . . .

Lord, teach me to pray. . . . Teach me to pray in faith. . . . Everyone that asks receives. Amen.

William Booth

He was a pawnbroker by day and a preacher by night. His day job gave him a window into the plight of the poor. He set up shop in a London slum under a tent on a burial ground that was no longer in use. Revival meetings were held there nightly for three straight weeks.

William Booth (1829–1912) came home one evening and told his wife, Catherine, "I have found my destiny." They rented an abandoned warehouse and called themselves the East London Revival Society. Their mission was to save souls and redeem the mass of suffering humanity drawn to London during the Industrial Revolution. William's battle cry was "Go for souls and go for the worst." They attracted the poor who felt unwelcome in conventional churches.

The society sang lively music. William often remarked, "Why should the devil have all the good music?" He preached using ordinary language, and people flocked to hear him like a rallied army. The society adopted the name Salvation Army quite by accident, but it suited them well. Their form of government was quasi-military. They wore uniforms, saluted a Christian flag, and appointed William general. They were ridiculed, yet they persevered as an army should.

William spoke to seven thousand salvationists three months before he died. The fire had still not gone out of him. "While women weep, as they do now, I'll fight; while children go hungry, as they do now, I'll fight; while men go to prison, in and out, in and out, as they do now, I'll fight; while there is a poor lost girl upon the streets, while there remains one dark soul without the light of God, I'll fight. I'll fight to the very end."

Thou Christ of burning, cleansing flame:
Send the fire!
Thy blood-bought gift today we claim:
Send the fire!
Look down and see this waiting host,
Give us the promised Holy Ghost,
We want another Pentecost:
Send the fire!

God of Elijah, hear our cry:
Send the fire!
And make us fit to live or die:
Send the fire!

To burn up every trace of sin,
To bring the light and glory in,
The revolution now begin:
Send the fire!

To make our weak hearts strong and brave:
Send the fire!
To live, a dying world to save:
Send the fire!

O see us on thy altar lay
Our lives, our all, this very day.
To crown the offering now we pray:
Send the fire!

Christina Rossetti

It hardly ever snows in the Holy Land, but you wouldn't know it by the lyrics of the Christmas carol "In the Bleak Midwinter," written by the highly esteemed poet Christina Rossetti (1830–1894). She was asked by the editor of *Scribner's Monthly* to submit a poem for inclusion in the literary periodical's January 1872 issue. She gave it an inauspicious title, "A Christmas Poem," that was changed thirty-four years later to its current title in hymn form.

Christina's poem is hardly a commentary on weather in Israel. Snow functions as a literary motif to juxtapose the barren, wintry conditions of humanity with the warmth of the Messiah's birth. Christ's arrival in the bleak midwinter when "earth stood hard as iron" alludes to the hardness of human hearts. The poem's middle stanzas move back and forth between Christ's divinity and humanity. The last stanza packs a punch. Shepherds can bring lambs and wise men can give expensive gifts, yet "what can I give him, poor as I am?" She answers her own introspective question with the simple words "Give my heart."

The somber mood of the carol correlates to Christina's real life. She struggled with chronic health issues and recurring bouts of depression. She received three marriage proposals yet turned them all down for various reasons. One suitor was described as a "sleepyhead," while another offended her antislavery sentiments. Her poems often contrast the inconstancy of human love and the vanity of earthly pleasures with God's enduring love.

The following prayer by Christina invites us to give our hearts to Christ.

O Lord, you see that all hearts are empty
unless you fill them,
and all desires are thwarted
unless they crave you.
Give us light and grace
to seek and find you,
that we may be yours
and you may be ours forever.
Amen.

Charles Spurgeon

Charles Spurgeon (1834–1892) was preaching strongly and passionately on the necessity of giving up every known sin that blocks true fellowship with God. He was sharing the preaching duties one evening with the Rev. Dr. George F. Pentecost, so he asked his friend to apply the principle he had just addressed in his sermon. George, who did not know that Charles smoked cigars, spoke at great length about the sin of cigar smoking. He told the congregation how he had struggled and finally succeeded in giving up this pernicious habit. When George finished, all eyes were on Charles since his cigar smoking was well known to the congregation. Charles stood and said with a playful smile, "Well, dear friends, you know that some men can do to the glory of God what to other men would be sin. And notwithstanding what Dr. Pentecost has said, I intend to smoke a good cigar to the glory of God before I go to bed tonight."

Charles Spurgeon was known as the "prince of preachers" in his day. He might be called the first megachurch pastor, having served the six-thousand-seat Metropolitan Tabernacle in London for thirty-eight years. While he was roundly criticized by the religious establishment for lacking a formal college education, he was in fact a voracious reader, consuming six books weekly and amassing a library of twelve thousand volumes.

One quality I admire about Charles is his candor in acknowledging his struggle with depression, called "melancholy" in nineteenth-century England and often viewed as a lack of faith. He reminded his people, "The strong are not always vigorous, the wise are not always ready, the brave are not always courageous, and the joyous are not always happy." A second quote from Charles makes me smile: "Is anyone altogether sane?" he asks. "Aren't we all a little off balance?" His short prayer on the opposite page reminds us not to allow any known sin room to grow in our hearts.

O my Savior, let me not fall little by little, or think myself able to bear the indulgence of any known sin because it seems so insignificant. Keep me from sinful beginnings, lest they lead me on to sorrowful endings.

Henry Guinness

People express surprise when they learn my family was in the brewing business for a hundred years. Making beer and delivering sermons don't belong together to most people. Yet the connection between beer and preaching would not have been viewed as strange by our spiritual forebears.

Henry Grattan Guinness (1835–1910) was born into a brewing family in Dublin, Ireland. He went to sea as a sailor and fell away from his childhood faith. He offered his life in full surrender to Christ at age twenty and became an itinerant evangelist, preaching the gospel in Scotland, England, Wales, France, Algeria, Egypt, Switzerland, China, Japan, and the US. His wife, Fanny, joined the ministry and took up preaching also. Later, they founded a missionary training school in London.

Henry was the grandson of Arthur Guinness, who started Guinness beer back in 1759. Author Os Guinness spoke at the church I served some years ago. Os hails from the same Guinness family and is Henry's great-grandson. Small world!

When I read Henry's sermons, I sensed his deep heart for evangelism. Every message in his collection of sermons ends with an appeal to come to Christ. He urges ministers to preach Christ and hearers to trust Christ. At the end of one sermon, he speaks about prayer, "Let your first prayer to Jesus, in the early childhood of your love to him, be 'Jesus, abide with me!' And when your hairs have grown gray in his service and the daylight fades around you, through the falling shadows, let this last prayer ascend to heaven—'Jesus, abide with me.'" This is one prayer Jesus is sure to answer.

Jesus, abide with me.
It is toward evening;
the day is far spent;
the night is at hand.
Jesus! through the twilight,
in the darkness,
at the daybreak,
in the glory,
and forever—
oh, abide—
Jesus, abide with me!

George Matheson

George Matheson (1842–1906) was loving life. He was an outstanding student at the University of Glasgow and newly engaged to be married. Then, his doctor delivered the fateful news that his degenerative eye condition was irreversible. George shared the news of his progressive blindness with his fiancée. She returned her engagement ring with a note: "I cannot see my way clear to go through life bound by the chains of marriage to a blind man." George was understandably devastated. His sister invited him to take up residence in her home, thereby making it possible for George to complete his studies. For years, she read the Bible to her brother and helped him prepare and practice his sermons. His preaching became known all over Scotland. Even Queen Victoria asked him to preach at her castle.

Fast-forward to 1882. George was forty years old, and it was the evening after his sister's wedding. He was alone at the house, and the wedding brought back painful reminders of his own broken engagement. A song formed in his head in a matter of minutes, as though it were being dictated to him: "O Love that wilt not let me go, I rest my weary soul in Thee . . ." A clause in the third stanza, "I trace the rainbow through the rain," is among my favorite one-liners in a hymn.

The following prayer is from a collection of devotional meditations George wrote, originally published in 1894.

Restore my soul, oh God! There are green pastures around me for which my eye has no lens, there are quiet waters beside me for which my ear has no chord; restore my soul. There are unknown beauties sleeping in every flower, there are unheard harmonies singing in every breeze; restore my soul. There are goodness and mercy following me in the valleys, there is a rod and a staff supporting me in all shadows; restore my soul. The path on which I go is already the path of your righteousness; open thou mine eyes, that I may behold its wonders. The place I call dreadful is even now the house of the Lord; the heavens shall cease to hide thee when thou hast restored my soul. Amen.

F. B. Meyer

How can I know God's will for my life? It's a question almost every believer asks. I met recently with seminary students seeking to answer this very question. How does God want me to use my seminary education to advance God's mission in the world?

Frederick Brotherton (F. B.) Meyer (1847–1929), who pastored several churches in England and later served as an itinerant evangelist, offered five practical suggestions for how to discern God's will in real life in his book *The Secret of Guidance*: (1) Examine your motives. Be alert to the subtle working of self-interest to distort your quest to do God's will. (2) Surrender your will. Jesus epitomized a surrendered life. Hand yourself completely over to God's direction in your life. (3) Exercise your mind to know God's will. God has given us remarkable cognitive powers to know his will through Scripture. (4) Be much in prayer. Put the matter squarely in God's hands. "When we want to know God's will, there are three things that need to line up: the inward impulse, the Word of God, and the trend of circumstances." (5) Wait for the gradual unfolding of God's plan in providence. If you do not know what to do, stand still. In the words of the prophet Habakkuk, "If the vision tarries, wait for it" (Hab. 2:3).

One more quote from Frederick: "God waits long enough to test patience of faith, but not a moment behind the extreme hour of need."

You may be wrestling with a major decision right now. Walk back through Frederick's five steps and utilize this prayer from his Exodus 3 devotion to relinquish your will to God's gracious intention for your life.

Some of us sorely need thee, O God. We have been disappointed many times in the things we thought would yield us profit and satisfaction. When we are most absorbed in our necessary business, may thy presence be manifested to us. May we realize that we are not wandering aimlessly upon the trackless desert, because thou art leading us. May every common bush be aflame with thee. Amen.

C. T. Studd

The Studd family (what a name!) were all superb cricket players. Cricket in nineteenth-century England was as popular as football has become in modern American culture. Edward Studd made a fortune importing tea from India and built a first-class cricket field in his own backyard. His three sons followed in his footsteps and became formidable cricket players. His youngest, Charles Thomas (C. T.) Studd (1860–1931) was the greatest of them all. He was named the best all-round cricket player in England for two consecutive years and elected captain of his Cambridge University team. He successfully led the team in upsetting the reigning world cricket champion, Australia, in 1883.

A year later, Charles's brother George became seriously ill, battling for his life. Charles realized as he kept vigil at his brother's bedside that his cricket career would soon be coming to an end. He wrote, "I know cricket will not last, and honor will not last, and nothing in this world will last, but it is worthwhile living for the world to come."

When he learned that the evangelist Dwight L. Moody was in town, Charles went to his crusade and fully surrendered his life to Jesus Christ. He gave away a sizable inheritance and became a missionary, as did his brother George (who recovered from his illness), in China, India, and Africa.

In 1912, Charles wrote a controversial pamphlet titled *The Chocolate Soldier*, challenging lukewarm Christians to become real soldiers for Christ, not chocolate soldiers who melt in the heat of battle. "We Christians today are a tepid crew," he said. He closed with the prayer that follows here. His language of "sleeping sickness" refers to reciting the Lord's Prayer without intending to do what we pray.

Good Lord!
Baptize us with the Holy Spirit, and with fire.
Cure us of all this dread plague of sleeping sickness,
this crazy talking in our sleep,
that even as we unceasingly pray,
thy name be hallowed everywhere,
thy kingdom come speedily,
thy will be done on earth as it is in heaven.
Amen and Amen!

Thomas Chisholm

Lamentations is likely not your favorite book in the Bible. Little wonder! It's a series of five laments over the destruction of Jerusalem and its temple by Babylonian invaders in 586 BC. Amid these laments, likely composed by the prophet Jeremiah, come the remarkable words "Because of the LORD's great love we are not consumed, for his compassions never fail. They are new every morning; great is your faithfulness" (Lam. 3:22–23 NIV). Perhaps a hymn is now playing in your head!

Thomas Obadiah Chisholm (1866–1960) was born and raised in a log cabin in rural Franklin, Kentucky. Although he never attended high school, he somehow managed to become a teacher. He was converted to Christ at a revival in his town and became a Methodist preacher. He lasted only one year in ministry due to poor health, and he moved to a farm with his wife and children to recuperate, facing unemployment and mounting health costs. He found work as an insurance agent and wrote poems on the side, eight hundred of which were published, and many of which were later set to music. In 1923 he sent a batch of poems to William M. Runyan, an editor at Hope Publishing Company in Chicago, who recognized potential in his "Great Is Thy Faithfulness." William wrote a tune for Thomas's text, and the hymn became a favorite at Billy Graham crusades.

Stanza 1 focuses on God's unchanging compassion: "There is no shadow of turning with Thee" and "Thou changest not, thy compassions, they fail not." In stanza 2, all of creation joins in praising God's faithfulness—summer, winter, springtime, harvest, sun, moon, stars. Stanza 3 celebrates God's compassion as "strength for today and bright hope for tomorrow," and the refrain reinforces the theme of God's faithfulness. Thomas said of the hymn, "Having been led, for part of my life, through some difficult periods, I have sought to gather from such experiences material out of which to write hymns of comfort and cheer for those similarly circumstanced." The hymn is addressed to God as a prayer.

Great is thy faithfulness, O God my Father;
There is no shadow of turning with thee;
Thou changest not, thy compassions, they fail not;
As thou hast been, thou forever wilt be.

Refrain:
Great is thy faithfulness!
Great is thy faithfulness!
Morning by morning new mercies I see;
All I have needed thy hand hath provided:
Great is thy faithfulness, Lord, unto me.

Summer and winter and springtime and harvest,
Sun, moon, and stars in their courses above,
Join with all nature in manifold witness
To thy great faithfulness, mercy, and love. [Refrain]

Pardon for sin and a peace that endureth,
Thine own dear presence to cheer and to guide,
Strength for today and bright hope for tomorrow:
Blessings all mine with ten thousand beside! [Refrain]

Amy Carmichael

Seven-year-old Preena went to draw water from a well. She overheard Amy Carmichael (1867–1951) telling women at the well about her God who loved everyone the same. This God did not assign people to different classes as did the Indian caste system. Preena's mother had sold her to a Hindu temple. A girl sold to the temple, called a *devadasi*, was married to the temple's god. Today we call it sex trafficking.

Preena resolved to live with this woman who spoke of God's love. She planned her escape in the middle of the night when her guardians were sleeping. She tiptoed quietly through an unlocked door and pushed open the heavy gate. Preena knocked at Amy's door and begged to come live with her. When Amy investigated the dark underworld of girls sold to the temple, she was horrified. There was no way Amy would hand Preena back over to that life. The temple priests came looking for Preena and accused Amy of kidnapping. Amy held her ground and adopted Preena. Suddenly, this single woman missionary from Ireland with no children of her own became *amma* (mother) to a seven-year-old.

Word spread, and more children showed up at Amy's doorstep. By 1904, three years later, Amy had become *amma* to seventeen more children.

Amy's mission to the children of India lasted fifty-five years. The Dohnavur Fellowship, led by Amy and later assisted by Preena, rescued a thousand children from similar bondage. Amy's prayer for children reflects her singular passion.

Father, hear us, we are praying,
Hear the words our hearts are saying,
We are praying for our children.

Keep them from the powers of evil,
From the secret, hidden peril,
From the whirlpool that would suck them,
From the treacherous quicksand pluck them.

From the worldling's hollow gladness,
From the sting of faithless sadness,
Holy Father, save our children.

Through life's troubled waters steer them,
Through life's bitter battle cheer them,
Father, Father, be Thou near them.

Read the language of our longing,
Read the wordless pleadings thronging,
Holy Father, for our children.

And whenever they may bide,
Lead them home at eventide.

Ida Scudder

She was so well known that a letter reached her addressed simply to "Dr. Ida, India." Ida Scudder (1870–1960) was born to American missionary parents in India. Her father was a missionary doctor, as was her grandfather, who left a thriving New York medical practice to enter the mission field in 1836. Forty-two members of the Scudder family over five generations have devoted 1,100 years to Christian medical missions in South India.

Ida initially had little interest in continuing in her father's footsteps. She preferred the educational comforts in the US but was called home to care for her ailing mother in India. A college friend said before she left, "You're going to become a missionary just like the rest of your family." Ida snapped back, "Oh no I won't. I will never be a missionary. You'll see. I'll be back in a year." Three different Indian men knocked at her parents' door one evening seeking medical attention for their distressed wives in labor. Their custom wouldn't allow a male doctor to treat their wives, so they refused her dad's help.

When Ida learned the next morning that all three women died in delivery, it stirred her to action. She sensed "God was calling me into his work" and enrolled at Cornell University in 1899, among the first class of women accepted into medical school. She opened a one-bed clinic in Vellore, South India, and two years later expanded it to a forty-bed hospital. She set up a roadside medical dispensary to provide care for remote villagers. When she needed additional staff, she opened a medical school for women nurses and medical doctors, unimaginable in those days. Today it's one of Asia's foremost teaching hospitals.

When asked about her ambitious plans for a medical school, Aunt Ida, as she was called, said, "First ponder, then dare. Know your facts. Count the cost. Money is not the important thing. What you are building is not a medical school. It is the kingdom of God. Don't err on the side of being too small." Her prayer leads us to meet today's challenges with like-minded confidence and gladness.

Father, whose love is within me and whose love is ever about me, grant that thy life may be maintained in my life today and every day; that with gladness of heart, without haste or confusion of thought, I may go about my daily tasks conscious of ability to meet every rightful demand, seeing the larger meaning of little things, and, finding beauty and love everywhere and in the sense of thy presence, may I walk through the hours breathing the atmosphere of love rather than anxious striving.

Thérèse of Lisieux

It was Christmas Eve, 1886. A fourteen-year-old girl attended midnight Mass with her family inside an enormous cathedral in France. Thérèse of Lisieux (1873–1897) was grieving her mother's recent death and was plagued with self-doubt. She wrote of worship that evening, "God worked a little miracle in me to grow up in an instant." She opened her heart to Christ and resolved to serve him.

She approached the bishop a year later to announce her intention to become a Carmelite nun. "You are only fifteen and you wish this?" the bishop asked. Her resolute response: "I wished it since the dawn of reason." And she convinced him to admit her six years before her she was eligible to join the Carmelite order. Some sisters looked down on her youth and bullied her. (I didn't know bullying was a problem in convents!) She lamented her littleness in age and unimportance but asked God for strength to serve "by the little way." She came to believe it wasn't necessary to accomplish some heroic act or great deed. She wrote, "The only way I can prove my love is by scattering flowers, and these flowers are every little sacrifice, every glance, and word, and the doing of the least actions for love."

Thérèse made her mark with her little way of love. Her resolve to fill every unpleasant moment and difficult circumstance with Christ's love became legendary to fellow sisters. She is best known for her spiritual autobiography, *The Story of a Soul*. As Thérèse demonstrated, it's not only the big things we do for God that matter; small deeds done with great conviction share God's heart with the world also. I am humbled by the simple prayer of this faithful woman who died at the tender age of twenty-four.

My life is but an instant, a passing hour.
My life is but a day that escapes and flies away.
O my God! You know that to love you on earth
I have only today!

Oh, I love you, Jesus! My soul yearns for you.
For just one day, remain my sweet support.
Come reign in my heart, give me your smile
Just for today!

. . . .

O, Divine Pilot! whose hand guides me,
I'm soon to see you on the eternal shore.
Guide my little boat over the stormy waves in peace
Just for today.

. . . .

Soon I'll fly away to speak your praises,
When the day without sunset will dawn on my soul.
Then I'll sing on the angels' lyre
The Eternal Today!

Evelyn Underhill

When my dad was alive, he liked to tell people I was the least likely person he had ever known to go into the ministry. I observe something similar regarding people I encounter in the church. Some of the least likely people become committed Christ followers while some of the more obvious candidates for faith never take it seriously.

Evelyn Underhill (1875–1941) could surely be classified as an unlikely Christian disciple. She was raised by parents indifferent to religion and had no formal religious training. She was agnostic in her early years, yet she also sensed the Divine in ways she couldn't explain. She dabbled in the occult before coming to faith after a trip to Italy and a visit to a convent. She became a leading voice for spiritual renewal in both Catholic and Anglican circles. She was the first woman to speak to an assembly of Anglican bishops. She led retreats and earned a reputation as an accomplished spiritual director. A letter was found recently among her papers that Evelyn sent to the archbishop of Canterbury (leader of the Anglican Communion). "People are hungry for God," she insisted, "not for institutional religion." She then commented on "the poor and shabby quality of the priests' inner life." She ended with an indictment of leading clergy of her day. "Their Christianity as a whole is humanitarian rather than theocentric." Gutsy words! Since the church's problems were primarily spiritual, not organizational, she counseled that what the church needed most was greater spiritual fervor and love for God. It was a shot over the bow for church leaders to cultivate an intentional life of prayer. Tell me, did she write this letter in 1930 or 2025?

She prays with similar courage in the following prayer.

Give me, O Lord, I beseech you,
courage to pray for light and to endure the light here
where I am in this world of yours,
which should reflect your beauty
but which we have spoiled and exploited.
Cast your radiance on the dark places,
those crimes and stupidities I like to ignore and gloss over.
Show up my pretensions,
my poor little claims and achievements,
my childish assumptions of importance,
my mock heroism.
Take me out of the confused half-light in which I live.
Enter and irradiate every situation and every relationship. . . .
Show me my opportunities,
the raw material of love, of sacrifice, of holiness,
lying at my feet,
disguised under homely appearance
and only seen as it truly is in your light.
Amen.

Robert Lawson

Robert C. Lawson (1883–1961) was orphaned at a young age and raised by an aunt, and he left home as a teenager to become a nightclub singer. He abandoned his Christian roots and adopted a pleasure-seeking lifestyle. At age thirty he contracted tuberculosis and was admitted to an Indianapolis hospital, sharing a room with a prize fighter whose mother insisted on praying for Robert's recovery. Doctors conceded Robert's prognosis was dire, given that he had tuberculosis in both lungs, but this "Holy Ghost woman" kept vigil for Robert.

After his dramatic improvement and release from the hospital, Robert was baptized and joined a Pentecostal church. God's presence came to him one night in audible form: "Go, preach my Word. I mean you. I mean you. I mean YOU. Go, preach my Word." Robert became an itinerant preacher and found his way to Harlem in 1919. The Holy Spirit prompted him to board the subway and follow the first man he saw, who led him to a prayer meeting. Long story short, Robert founded a church that became known as the Refuge Church of Christ, which he served until his death in 1961.

Robert possessed a curious blend of Pentecostal theology and passion for social change, a rarity in those days. He opened a funeral home that charged only modest fees, a grocery store in his church to assist low-income people, and schools for inner-city youth. He ministered during the era of Jim Crow and the "one-drop rule," by which anyone with a trace of Black ancestry was considered Black and was therefore disqualified from the privileges accorded to whites. Robert wrote in *The Anthropology of Jesus Christ Our Kinsman* that according to the one-drop rule, Jesus would be considered Black, since the blood of all nations flowed in his veins. Robert believed the color line was something Christ obliterated, as expressed in Paul's assertion in his letter to the Romans that nothing can separate us from the love of Christ (Rom. 8:35–39).

It's instructive that the four Gospel writers never provide a description of what Jesus looked like. The omission is striking when you consider the tendency of first-century Greco-Roman biographers to include elaborate descriptions of people's physical characteristics. Jesus unites all people in his own ancestral bloodline.

O God, who has made humanity in thine own likeness, and who doth love all whom thou hast made, suffer us not because of difference of race, color, or condition to separate ourselves from others and thereby from thee; but teach us the unity of thy family and the universality of thy love. As thou, Savior, as a son, was born of a Hebrew mother, who had the blood of many nations in her veins, and ministered first to thy brethren of the Israelites, but rejoiced in the faith of a Syro-Phoenician woman and a Roman soldier, and suffered your cross to be carried by an Ethiopian, teach us also, while loving and serving our own, to enter into the communion of the whole human family, and forbid that from pride of birth, color, achievement, and hardness of heart, we should despise any for whom Christ died, or injure or grieve any in whom he lives. We pray in Jesus' precious name. Amen.

Helen Keller

Anne Sullivan went to live with the Kellers in Alabama as Helen Keller's (1880–1968) teacher. The story of Anne's tutelage of Helen has been well documented, a relationship that spanned forty-nine years.

Anne and Helen traveled to Boston's Perkins School for the Blind and visited with Phillips Brooks, a well-known pastor most remembered for conducting Abraham Lincoln's funeral and writing the words of the Christmas carol "O Little Town of Bethlehem." Phillips, who never married and had no family of his own, loved children and agreed to Helen's request to correspond with her. She was only ten years old when she initiated correspondence with Phillips (her handwriting was flawless), peppering him with questions, such as, "Why does the dear Father in heaven think it best for us to have very great sorrow sometimes?" She ended the letter, "Please tell me something that you know about God. It makes me happy to know about my loving Father who is good and wise. I hope you will write to your little friend when you have time." Phillips sent a response from London, attempting to answer her questions, and concluded, "I love to tell you about God. But He will tell you Himself by the love which He will put into your heart if you ask Him. And, Jesus, who is His Son, . . . came into the world on purpose to tell us all about the Father's love. If you read His words, you will see how full His heart is of the love of God. . . . Though men were very cruel to Him and at last killed Him, He was willing to die for them because He loved them so." What Helen said to him in a follow-up visit is a keeper: "Mr. Brooks, I always knew He was there, but I didn't know His name."

Helen's prayer for peace in 1936 is so relevant to our time.

O Lord, in whose countenance is the morning of all things made new, shine upon us that we may illumine with peace the world-home thou hast given us. Remove from us pride of might and arrogance of possession. Stretch our thoughts, O Divine Mind, that we may see the whole earth as our country, and the inhabitants thereof as our neighbors. Fill our hearts with love that changes discord to trust.

Temper to our good the weariness and the broken hopes we cannot escape. Pour into us the strength of all valiant spirits. Put into our hands constructive tasks of peace. Let not our striving end with condemnation of folly and stupidity in high places.

Quicken in us the will to resist the hysteria that they who take the sword raise to turn us aside from thy commandments. Give us power to the depth, breadth, and height of our souls to prevent the destructions we have lived to weep. Out of the embers of fires that have scorched and blackened thy kingdom on earth, help us create a new order in which we will no more become savages through fear. Unite us, millions strong, against the darkness of hate, as unnumbered sunbeams streaming one way sweeten the sod unto green ecstasy and fruitfulness.

John Baillie

There are head people and heart people. Head people think deeply and analyze thoroughly. Heart people feel intensely and empathize easily. Some think with their heads; others lead with their hearts. It is rare to find people who can put head and heart together.

John Baillie (1886–1960) may be one such person. He was a theology professor at Edinburgh University in Scotland and several seminaries in the States. He thought deeply about God and wrote big books about theology. He probed the profound mysteries of the faith and researched the Bible with consummate skill. Yet he also had a heartfelt connection to God and was devoted to prayer.

While John wrote widely on theological subjects, the book for which he is most remembered is *A Diary of Private Prayer*. First published in 1936, it remains an enduring Christian devotional with more than a million copies in print. He arranged his diary as a series of morning and evening prayers for each day of the month. He believed the best way to learn to pray is by praying.

The prayer that follows is the morning prayer for day 27. I urge you not to hurry through it. Take time with its words and let them lead you into conversation with God. I'm drawn to these three sentences: "Give me a stout heart to bear my own burdens. Give me a willing heart to bear the burdens of others. Give me a believing heart to cast all burdens upon Thee." In a short span, we pray to bear up under our burdens, carry each other's burdens, and give all burdens to God.

Grant, O most gracious God, that I may carry with me through this day's life
the remembrance of the sufferings and death of Jesus Christ my Lord.

For thy fatherly love shown forth in Jesus Christ thy well-beloved Son:
For his readiness to suffer for our sakes:
For the redemptive passion that filled his heart:
I praise and bless thy holy name.

For the power of his cross in the history of the world since he came:
For all who have taken up their own crosses and have followed him:
For the noble army of martyrs and for all who are willing to die that others
    may live:
For all suffering freely chosen for noble ends, for pain bravely endured, for
    temporal sorrows that have been used for the building up of eternal joys:
I praise and bless thy holy name.

O Lord my God, who dwellest in pure and blessed serenity beyond the reach
    of mortal pain,
yet lookest down in unspeakable love and tenderness upon the sorrows of earth,
give me grace, I beseech thee,
to understand the meaning of such afflictions and disappointments as I
    myself am called upon to endure.
Deliver me from all fretfulness.
Let me be wise to draw from every dispensation of thy providence the lesson
    thou art minded to teach me.
Give me a stout heart to bear my own burdens.
Give me a willing heart to bear the burdens of others.
Give me a believing heart to cast all burdens upon thee.

Glory be to thee, O Father, and to thee, O Christ, and to thee, O Holy
    Spirit, forever and ever. Amen.

Karl Barth

History has shown that church-run states don't work. Neither do state-run churches. Nazi leadership took control of the German Evangelical Church in 1933. Clergy were pressured to preach the superiority of the Aryan race and espouse Nazi ideology. A group of pastors came together in 1934 to oppose the Nazi takeover of the church, adopted the name the Confessing Church, and formulated a written rebuttal.

The primary architect of the resolution was Karl Barth (1886–1968), a theology professor at the University of Bonn. He composed the draft on a Sunday evening, fortified by strong coffee and Brazilian cigars. While there is much to commend in this statement, I'll limit myself to a single sentence: "We reject the false doctrine that there could be areas of our life in which we would not belong to Jesus Christ but to other lords." Translated, it means Jesus is Lord and Hitler is not. Karl sent a personal copy of the finished product, the Barmen Declaration, to Hitler himself. He was forced to resign his professorship for refusing to sign an oath of allegiance to Hitler. He returned to his native Switzerland to teach theology at the University of Basel and continued his support of the Confessing Church.

Karl was trained under liberal theology but was dismayed at its moral weakness and became decidedly more orthodox in his later years. He came to America on a lecture tour in 1962. When speaking at the University of Chicago, he was asked in a Q&A session if he could summarize his theological work in a sentence. "Yes, I can," he said. "In the words of the song I learned at my mother's knee, 'Jesus loves me, this I know, for the Bible tells me so.'"

Karl composed prayers as well as major theological works. The following prayer is from his book *Fifty Prayers*.

Lord our God, when we are afraid, do not permit us to doubt!
When we are disappointed, let us not become bitter!
When we have fallen, do not leave us lying down!
When we have come to the end of our understanding and our powers,
    do not leave us to die!
No, let us then feel your nearness and your love,
that you have promised to those whose hearts are humble and broken,
and who fear your Word.
Amen.

Reinhold Niebuhr

It may be the most popular prayer of our modern era. Reinhold Niebuhr (1892–1971), a theology professor at Union Theological Seminary in New York City, preached a sermon at Heath Union Church in Massachusetts in 1943. He concluded the sermon by praying what has become known as the Serenity Prayer. He had prayed variations of it in public before, but this time it really seemed to stick.

The prayer circulated quickly. An emerging twelve-step recovery program called Alcoholics Anonymous (AA) featured it prominently in its literature. It was included in a book of prayers for US Army chaplains to use in World War II. Today, the Serenity Prayer has become ubiquitous in popular culture.

The genius of the prayer is its ability to distill three essential truths with profound simplicity. The first principle, "Give me grace to accept with serenity the things that cannot be changed," serves as an antidote to chronic worry and anxiety. The middle section, "courage to change the things that should be changed," shifts from serene acceptance to resolute reform. The last portion, "and the wisdom to distinguish the one from the other," asks for God's discernment to know when to practice acceptance versus courage.

God, give us grace to accept with serenity
The things that cannot be changed,
Courage to change the things
That should be changed,
And the wisdom to distinguish
The one from the other.

Dorothy Sayers

She worked for a London ad agency by day, writing jingles for Colman's mustard and Guinness beer. She coined the phrase "It pays to advertise." By night, Dorothy L. Sayers (1893–1957) wrote mystery novels during the male-dominated golden age of British detective fiction in the 1920s and '30s. She made her debut with the novel *Whose Body?* in 1923. It was the beginning of the Lord Peter Wimsey detective series, and she cranked out twelve novels in a span of fourteen years. In 1937 she was asked to write a play to be performed in church. *Zeal for Thy House* was a popular and controversial drama that took aim at lukewarm Christianity. It thrust this successful detective writer into the religious world.

Dorothy was repeatedly asked about her Christian faith, and she responded with an article that appeared in the British *Sunday Times*, "The Greatest Drama Ever Staged Is the Official Creed of Christendom." She insisted that the story of Christianity is the most remarkable of tales, but the church has tamed and subdued it. She wrote, "Let us, in Heaven's name, drag out the Divine Drama from under the dreadful accumulation of slipshod thinking and trashy sentiment heaped upon it, and set it on an open stage to startle the world into some sort of vigorous reaction. If the pious are the first to be shocked, so much the worse for the pious—others will pass into the Kingdom of Heaven." She devoted much of the second half of her writing career to informing readers that Jesus is far more substantial and subversive than the church of her day recognized.

She wrote "Hymn in Contemplation of Sudden Death," which first appeared in *Oxford Magazine*. Six of its nine stanzas form the prayer that follows.

God, if this day my journey end,
I thank You first for many a friend,
The sturdy and unquestioned piers
That run beneath my bridge of years.

. . . .

Next for the joy of labor done
And burdens shouldered in the sun,
Not less, for shame of labor lost,
And meekness born of barren boast.

For every fair and useless thing
That bids us pause from laboring,
To look and find the larkspur blue
And marigolds of a different hue.

For eyes to see and ears to hear,
For tongue to speak and news to bear,
For hands to handle, feet to go,
For life, I give You thanks also.

For all things merry, quaint, and strange,
For sound and silence, strength, and change,
At last, for death, which only gives
Value to everything that lives.

For these, good God, who still makes me,
I praise Your name, since, verily,
I of my joy have had no dearth,
Though this day were my last on earth.

Fulton Sheen

An eight-year-old altar boy was assigned to assist a bishop in serving the Eucharist. He dropped the container holding the wine (called a cruet) on the floor and it shattered. After Communion, the bishop sought out the frightened boy and made two bold predictions: he will study at the esteemed Catholic University of Leuven in Belgium, and "someday you will be as I am."

Both predictions came true. Peter John Sheen (1895–1979), who went by the name Fulton, graduated with a PhD from the Catholic University of Leuven and became a bishop (and later archbishop). He taught at the Catholic University of America in Washington, DC, but was best known for his ministry in radio and television. He hosted the popular *Catholic Hour* radio show from 1930 to 1950 and then switched to television, hosting his own network series, *Life Is Worth Living*, from 1952 to 1957. I am old enough to remember watching him on TV. I hadn't a clue that his distinctive cape and beanie were religious vestments. His program generated 8,500 weekly letters. He received an Emmy for the Most Outstanding Television Personality in the inaugural year of his unscripted show. He said in his acceptance speech, "In accepting this award, I feel it is time I pay tribute to my four writers: Matthew, Mark, Luke, and John."

There are so many memorable quotes attributed to Bishop Fulton Sheen. Two stand out for me: "Sometimes the only way the good Lord can get into some hearts is to break them," and "If you don't behave as you believe, you will end up believing as you behave." He taught Catholics and Protestants alike to pray using honest, everyday language. When it comes to making petitions to God, he suggested praying in a format like this.

Dear Lord,
there is something I want, I need badly.
I hope I want it for Thy glory
and it's best for my salvation.
You know what I wish.
Maybe it is not good for me,
or You would have given it to me long before this.
Just in case You are waiting for me to ask again,
well, I am.
You know best what to do.
Thanks.

Thomas Dorsey

Why don't we tell the stories that accompany the hymns we sing? Virtually every song has a story to accompany it. So many hymns emerge out of pain and intense struggle. Once you know the story behind the hymn "Precious Lord, Take My Hand," you'll never sing it the same way again.

Thomas A. Dorsey (1899–1993) was a well-known jazz and blues arranger and singer who turned his interest to Black gospel music. He traveled to St. Louis in 1932 to sing at a large revival meeting while his wife, Nettie, eight months pregnant, stayed behind in Chicago. After Thomas finished singing, he was handed a telegram that read, "Your wife just died." He rushed home only to find that his newborn son had also died that same evening. "I felt God had done me an injustice," Thomas wrote later. "I didn't want to serve him anymore or write gospel songs." OK, I've never said it quite that way before, but I've felt it sometimes.

A week later, Thomas sat down at the piano and began to improvise on an old Sunday school tune. The words began to flow as he poured out his lament to God in song. He composed a song that he shared with the music director of Atlanta's Ebenezer Baptist Church. The next Sunday, the choir sang "Precious Lord, Take My Hand." In Thomas's words, it "tore up the church." The pastor, Dr. Martin Luther King Sr., fell in love with the song. So did his famous son, at whose funeral it was sung.

Precious Lord, take my hand,
Lead me on, let me stand;
I am tired, I am weak, I am worn.
Through the storm, through the night,
Lead me on to the light:
Take my hand, precious Lord, lead me home.

When my way grows drear,
Precious Lord, linger near;
When my life is almost gone,
Hear my cry, hear my call,
Hold my hand lest I fall:
Take my hand, precious Lord, lead me home.

When the darkness appears,
And the night draws near,
And the day is past and gone,
At the river I stand,
Guide my feet, hold my hand:
Take my hand, precious Lord, lead me home.

Watchman Nee

A dramatic shift is well underway. The influence of Christianity is declining in the US, much as it has in Europe in recent years. Yet the number of Christian converts has been surging in Africa, Latin America, and Asia. The church in China is flourishing.

Nobody saw this coming when Western missionaries were expelled from China in the early 1950s. The witness of Chinese believers like Ni Tuosheng (Watchman Nee) (1903–1972) fortified the church against Communist persecution. When Mao Zedong came to power in 1949, he arrested outspoken Christians like Watchman, whom he sentenced to fifteen years in prison. A fellow prisoner who was later released testified to the impact Uncle Nee had on his life. This prisoner referenced the Chinese idiom that education by word is less effective than education by action. He saw faith in action in Uncle Nee and became a committed Christian.

Watchman should have been released in 1967, but the Cultural Revolution intervened and he was sent to a distant labor camp, where he died after twenty years in prison. He left a note under his pillow that read, "Christ is the Son of God and died for the redemption of sins and resurrected after three days. This is the greatest truth in the universe. I die because of my belief in Christ." Watchman wrote of prayer, "Our prayers lay the track upon which God's power can come. Like a mighty locomotive, his power is irresistible, but it cannot reach us without rails." God is not limited to our prayers, but God chooses to work cooperatively with prayer.

Watchman struggled with tuberculosis earlier in life as he was translating the works of Francis of Assisi. In response to his illness and inspired by St. Francis, he wrote the following prayer-poem, "Ràng wǒ ài ér bù shòu gǎndài," which was later set to music and translated from Chinese to English.

Let me love and not be requited.
Let me serve and not be rewarded.
Let me labor and not be remembered.
Let me suffer and not be regarded.

Let me pour wine, while I drink not.
Let me break bread, while I keep not,
Pour my life that others be blessed,
Be in suff'ring that they be contented.

None to pity or care for me,
None to praise me or to console me.
I would rather be desolate, wretched,
Lonely, friendless, and wrongly treated.

With my blood and tears pay the price to gain the crown,
Suffer loss that I might a pilgrim's life live out.
For, Lord, this is how You lived Your life
When You walked on this earthly sphere:
Gladly bore all loss that those who drew near
Could be freed from all suffering and fear.

I know not how far the future lies ahead.
On this path of no retreating, I am led.
So, Lord, let me now learn from Your perfect pattern,
Suff'ring wrong, no resentment in return.

May You in this difficult, tedious day,
All my tears shed in secret wipe away.
Let me learn You are my only solacement,
And let my life for others' joy be spent.

Alan Paton

Of all the Washington, DC, monuments, the Lincoln Memorial is my favorite, anchoring one end of the National Mall. Excerpts from Lincoln's Gettysburg Address and his second inaugural speech are engraved on its marble walls. Lincoln is seated in the center, a commanding presence, the burdens of America's Civil War etched in his face.

Alan Paton (1903–1988) visited the Lincoln Memorial in 1946 as he was writing his groundbreaking novel, *Cry, the Beloved Country*. The story is set in Alan's homeland of South Africa, ruled in those days by strict racial separation called apartheid. He wrote about his visit to the monument, "I mounted the steps of the Lincoln Memorial with a feeling akin to awe, and stood there a long time before the seated figure of one of the greatest men of history, surely the greatest of all the rulers of nations, the man who would spend a sleepless night because he had been asked to order the execution of a young soldier. He certainly knew that in pardoning we are pardoned."

Alan's novel became a national bestseller, controversial in South Africa for its vigorous opposition to apartheid. The storyline follows two men, one Black and one white, bound together by murder and the power of repentance and forgiveness. The book is full of biblical allusions. The main protagonists, with biblical names, are earnest Christians. Christian themes of suffering, forgiveness, and hope play a prominent role.

Alan wrote other books, including *Instrument of Thy Peace*, a series of twenty-one meditations on the prayer attributed to Francis of Assisi, "Lord, make me an instrument of your peace." It features several written prayers of his own, including this one.

O Lord, open my eyes that I may see the need of others.
Open my ears that I may hear their cries.
Open my heart so that they need not be without succor.
Let me not be afraid to defend the weak because of the anger of the strong,
nor afraid to defend the poor because of the anger of the rich.
Show me where love and hope and faith are needed,
and use me to bring them to those places.
And so open my eyes and my ears
that I may this coming day be able to do some work of peace for Thee.
Amen.

Malcolm Muggeridge

I doubt you would have cared much for Malcolm Muggeridge (1903–1990) in the first six decades of his life. He was known as a cutting-edge British journalist who skewered victims with biting sarcasm. He harangued the church as a hardened atheist. He was infatuated with communism until he went to Moscow on assignment and witnessed the brutality of Stalin's totalitarian regime. Worse yet, he was a hard-drinking, chain-smoking womanizer. That's why he titled his autobiography *Chronicles of Wasted Time*.

So why am I writing about him in this book of prayers? Because the change that came over him turned his life upside down. As a television personality who interviewed famous people, his visit with Mother Teresa rocked his world. No one had ever heard of Mother Teresa before Malcolm interviewed her. He was so taken with her that he spearheaded a documentary film on her work that was later published in book form, *Something Beautiful for God*.

In the early 1970s, Malcolm began to identify himself as a Christian. He wrote three books in quick succession about Jesus and walked away from his former life. His decision to quit drinking and philandering stunned English society. He and his wife, Kitty, joined the Roman Catholic Church in 1982, no doubt as a result of Mother Teresa's influence. He wrote of joining the church that he felt "a sense of homecoming, of picking up the threads of a lost life, of responding to a bell that had long been ringing, of taking a place at a table that had long been vacant."

Written two years before he died, his last book, *Conversion: The Spiritual Journey of a Twentieth-Century Pilgrim*, includes this prayer.

God, humble my pride,
extinguish the last stirrings of my ego,
obliterate whatever remains of worldly ambition and carnality,
and help me to serve only Thy purposes,
to speak and write only Thy words,
to think only Thy thoughts,
to have no other prayer than "Thy will be done."

Dietrich Bonhoeffer

Hitler's takeover of the German Evangelical Church was resisted by a small number of dissenting pastors like Dietrich Bonhoeffer (1906–1945). Dietrich challenged his pastoral colleagues to stand for Christ and not succumb to Hitler's fear tactics. The seminary Dietrich led was closed by the Gestapo in 1937. A year later, German pastors were ordered to swear an oath of allegiance to Hitler. Dietrich's friends helped him flee to America in 1939.

After two weeks in New York, he announced to the seminary sponsoring him, "I have come to the conclusion that I made a mistake in coming to America. I must live through this difficult period of our national history with the Christian people of Germany. I have no right to participate in the reconstruction of Christian life in Germany after the war if I do not share the trials of this time with my people." He returned to Germany on the last scheduled steamer to cross the Atlantic.

Dietrich was forbidden to speak in public and ostensibly went to work for the German military intelligence office. In reality, he continued his resistance work against the Nazis and was arrested in 1943. He wrote a letter from prison that he never regretted his decision to return to Germany. "You must never doubt that I'm traveling with gratitude and cheerfulness along the road where I'm being led," he wrote. "My past life is brimful of God's goodness, and my sins are covered by the forgiving love of Christ crucified."

Just eleven days before Allied forces liberated Europe in 1945, Dietrich Bonhoeffer was executed. Had he stayed in New York, America might have gained a theologian, but our world would have lost a martyr for peace and justice. Martin Luther said, "To go against conscience is neither right nor safe." Dietrich was a man of conscience. A book compiled after his death, *Letters and Papers from Prison*, includes this prayer.

Lord God, misery has come over me. My afflictions are about to crush me; I don't know which way to turn. God, be gracious and help me. Give me strength to bear what you send. Do not let fear rule over me. Give fatherly care to those I love, especially my wife and children; protect them with your strong hand from evil and all danger.

Merciful God, forgive me everything in which I have sinned against you and others. I trust in your grace and commit my life entirely into your hand. Do with me as pleases you and as is good for me. Whether I live or die, I am with you and you are with me, my God. Lord, I await your salvation and your kingdom. Amen.

Mother Teresa

Americans voted her the most admired woman of the twentieth century. When the personal letters and papers of Mary Teresa Bojaxhiu (1910–1997), better known as Mother Teresa, were published in 2007, the book took everyone by surprise. *Come, Be My Light* chronicles her fifty-year struggle with doubt and depression.

Early in her ministry as a nun, Mother Teresa felt a deep connection with Jesus. She experienced repeated visions of Jesus calling her to begin her Missionaries of Charity work. She became easily recognizable, dressed in her distinctive blue and white habit, caring for poor, abandoned children. We admired her loving manner and resilient generosity.

So, what are we to make of her letters, which she never wanted to make public, that describe her acute desolation? Some conjecture she suffered from depression. The telltale signs of it are evident in her words about darkness and loneliness. The fact that her misery didn't respond to pastoral counseling or staying busy with work could be an indicator of clinical depression. Others explained her affliction in spiritual terms, in what John of the Cross called a "dark night of the soul." Her letters reveal a decades-long struggle with doubt and dryness in prayer.

Perhaps her struggles were both physical and spiritual. We want to place our spiritual leaders on superhero pedestals. It's official now—Mother Teresa is not a plaster-of-Paris saint. Her perseverance in serving the Lord, despite mental distress, wins my admiration. It makes her more believable and accessible. Faith can coexist with doubt. Jesus commended the man who exclaimed, "Lord, I believe; help thou mine unbelief" (Mark 9:24 KJV). The prayer Mother Teresa prayed daily, an adaptation of a John Henry Newman prayer, becomes more powerful, given what we know about her now.

Dear Jesus, help us to spread your fragrance everywhere we go.
Flood our souls with your spirit and life.
Penetrate and possess our whole being so utterly
that our lives may only be a radiance of yours.

Shine through us and be so in us
that every soul we come in contact with
may feel your presence in our soul.
Let them look up and see no longer us, but only Jesus.

Stay with us, and then we shall begin to shine as you shine,
so to shine as to be light to others.
The light, O Jesus, will be all from you.
None of it will be ours.

It will be you shining on others through us.
Let us thus praise you in the way you love best,
by shining on those around us.
Let us preach you without preaching:
not by words, but by our example,
by the catching force—
the sympathetic influence of what we do,
the evident fullness of the love our hearts bear to you.
Amen.

Madeleine L'Engle

I have long appreciated the writing of Madeleine L'Engle (1918–2007) and particularly her words about prayer. So you can imagine my surprise when I read that her novel *A Wrinkle in Time* has consistently appeared on the list of most frequently banned books. Madeleine took heat from both sides: secular as well as religious. The secular set labeled her books as too religious for quoting the Bible so often and giving hints of her Christian leanings. The religious crowd took exception to the magical elements in her book. Does the brouhaha some years ago over the *Harry Potter* series ring a bell? Some actually claimed she promoted an occultic worldview. Geez. Give the woman a break!

I am indebted to Madeleine for something she wrote about prayer that finally pushed me over the edge to incorporate prayer into my daily life: "Praying is like playing the piano. You won't do it well every single day, but unless you do it every single day, you're never going to do it well." Madeleine wrote the following prayer while riding the 104 Broadway bus in New York City.

There is too much pain
I cannot understand
I cannot pray

. . . .

Here I am
and the ugly man with beery breath beside me reminds me that it is not my
    prayers that waken your concern, my Lord;
my prayers, my intercessions are not to ask for your love
for all your lost and lonely ones,
your sick and sinning souls,
but mine, my love, my acceptance of your love.
Your love for the woman sticking her umbrella and her expensive parcels
    into my ribs and snarling, "Why don't you watch where you are going?"
Your love for the long-haired, gum-chewing boy who shoves the old lady
    aside to grab a seat.
Your love for me, too, too tired to look with love,
too tired to look at Love, at you, in every person on the bus.
Expand my love, Lord, so I can help to bear the pain . . .

Joseph Bayly

Surgeon General C. Everett Koop attended the funeral for his friend's eighteen-year-old son, who died in a sledding accident. The surgeon general, whose own college-age son had died in a rock-climbing accident, recalls the moment in the service when his friend Joe went forward to speak about his son. He writes, "Joe Bayly went to the front of the church. The lump in Joe's throat was so large he could barely talk. But he did, and his opening words are burned forever in my mind: 'I want to speak to you today about my earthly son and his heavenly Father.'" Joe and his wife, Mary Lou, had already lost two sons to death—one at eighteen days following surgery, and another at five years from leukemia.

I first became acquainted with Joseph Bayly (1920–1986) from his book *A View from the Hearse: A Christian View of Death*, also published under the title *The Last Thing We Talk About*. I was a recent seminary grad and just starting out in a new pastoral call when I read his book to receive help in ministering to grieving people. His candor in writing about grief from the vantage point of a dad who lost three sons remains with me after all these years. I still recall one sentence from his book: "Don't forget in the darkness what you have learned in the light."

Joe also wrote a book of prayers titled *Psalms of My Life*. One of those prayers, "A Psalm of Single-Mindedness," follows here.

Lord of reality, make me real,
not plastic, synthetic, pretend, phony,
an actor playing a part, a hypocrite.
I don't want to keep a prayer list;
I want to pray.
I don't want to agonize to find your will;
I want to obey what I already know.
I don't want to argue theories of inspiration;
I want to submit to your word.
I don't want to explain the difference between eros *and* philos
and agape;
I want to love.
I don't want to sing as if I mean it;
I want to mean it.
I don't want to just tell it like it is;
I want to be it like you want it.
I don't want to think another needs me;
I want to know I need them or else I'm not complete.
I don't want to tell others how to do it;
I want to do it.
I don't want to have to always be right;
I want to admit it when I'm wrong.
I don't want to be insensitive;
I want to hurt where other people hurt.
I don't want to say, "I know how you feel";
I want to say, "God knows, and I'll try if you'll be patient with me, and
meanwhile, I'll be quiet."
I don't want to scorn the clichés of others;
I want to mean everything I say,
including this.

Henri Nouwen

Adam Arnett never spoke a word in his life. He couldn't dress himself or walk on his own, and he was susceptible to daily seizures. Yet he had a profound influence on Henri Nouwen (1932–1996), one of the most respected Catholic teachers and writers of the twentieth century. Henri taught at leading universities: Notre Dame, Yale, and Harvard. He turned out a book a year. He traveled the globe as a highly sought-after conference speaker. And it just about killed him. The frenetic schedule was suffocating his spiritual life.

So in 1985, he shocked the scholarly world by leaving academia to become a priest-in-residence at L'Arche, a residence for intellectually disabled adults outside Toronto. He was assigned to work with Adam as part of his new pastoral calling. Henri spent two hours each morning bathing, dressing, and feeding Adam. Was it the best use of a busy priest's time? Couldn't someone else take care of these menial chores? Listen to what Henri said about it: "I'm not the one giving up anything. It is I, not Adam, who gets the main benefit from our friendship." In the process of caring for Adam, he gained a fresh perspective on what it means to be loved by God. Henri lived at L'Arche and cared for Adam for eleven years until Adam's death in 1996. Henri was working on a book about Adam when he died later that same year. Its title wouldn't surprise you: *Adam—God's Beloved*. We need to stop our endless striving and rest in God's love.

Another book by Henri, *A Cry for Mercy*, contains six months' worth of prayers intended to help us live each day in the presence of God. One of them is excerpted on the following page.

O Lord, life passes by swiftly. Events that a few years ago kept me totally preoccupied have become vague memories; conflicts that only a few months ago seemed so crucial in my life now seem futile and hardly worth the energy; inner turmoil that robbed me of my sleep only a few weeks ago has now become a strange emotion of the past; books that filled me with amazement a few days ago now do not seem nearly as important; thoughts which kept my mind captive only a few hours ago have now lost their power and have been replaced by others.

Why is it so hard to learn from these insights? Why am I continually trapped by a sense of urgency and emergency? Why do I not see that you are eternal, that your kingdom lasts forever, and that for you a thousand years are like one day? O Lord, let me enter into your presence and there taste the eternal, timeless, everlasting love with which you invite me to let go of my time-bound anxieties, fears, preoccupations, and worries. . . .

Lord, teach me your ways and give me the courage to follow them. Amen.

Sources

These sources of the prayers appear in alphabetical order by author name.

ALCUIN OF YORK. Lightly edited from J. Manning Potts, ed., *Prayers of the Middle Ages* (Nashville: Upper Room, 1908).

ALFRED, KING OF WESSEX. King Alfred appended this prayer to the end of his Old English translation of Boethius's *De consolatione philosophiae* (On the Consolation of Philosophy). The modern English translation given here is lightly adapted from the uncredited one in *A Chain of Prayer across the Ages: Forty Centuries of Prayer, 2000 B.C.–A.D. 1915*, ed. Selina Fitzherbert Fox (London: John Murray, 1915), 133.

RICHARD ALLEN. This prayer is a condensed version of Richard Allen's "Acts of Faith" that accompanied the establishment of the African Methodist Episcopal Church in 1821. It is contained in *The Life, Experience, and Gospel Labours of Rt. Rev. Richard Allen* (Philadelphia: Martin & Boden, 1833).

AMBROSE OF MILAN. Lightly edited from *A Manual of Prayers for the Use of the Catholic Laity: The Official Prayer Book of the Catholic Church*, prepared and published by the Order of the Third Plenary Council of Baltimore (New York: Christian Press Association, 1896), 315–16. See also J. Manning Potts, ed., *Prayers of the Early Church* (Nashville: Upper Room, 1908).

ANSELM OF CANTERBURY. From Anselm, *Proslogion*, chap. 1, in *St. Anselm: Proslogium; Monologium; An Appendix In Behalf of the Fool by Gaunilon; and Cur Deus Homo*, translated from the Latin by Sidney Norton Deane (La-Salle, IL: Open Court, 1903), 3–6. Lightly edited.

THOMAS ARNOLD. "Prayer Read Every Morning in the Sixth Form," in Arthur Penrhyn Stanley, *The Life and Correspondence of Thomas Arnold* (New York: Charles Scribner's Sons, 1903), 299.

ANTHONY ASHLEY-COOPER, 7TH EARL OF SHAFTESBURY. From a diary entry dated June 1, 1846, quoted in *The Life and Work of the Seventh Earl of Shaftesbury, K.G.* by Edwin Hodder (London: Cassell, 1890), 357.

ATHANASIUS. Attributed to Athanasius, this prayer is preserved in a tenth-century manuscript: British Library, Or. 7029, fols. 65r–65v. This English translation from the original Coptic is by E. A. (Ernest Alfred) Wallis Budge and appears in *Miscellaneous Coptic Texts in the Dialect of Upper Egypt*, vol. 5 (London: British Museum, 1915), 1017–18.

AUGUSTINE OF HIPPO. Lightly edited from *The Confessions of S. Augustine*, translated from the Latin by the Rev. E. B. (Edward Bouverie) Pusey (Oxford: John Henry Parker, 1853), 10.38.

JOHN BAILLIE. John Baillie, *A Diary of Private Prayer* (New York: Scribner's Sons, 1949), 113.

ALBERT BARNES. Lightly edited from Albert Barnes, *A Manual of Prayer: Designed to Assist Christians in Learning the Subjects and Modes of Devotion*, 2nd ed. (Philadelphia: Henry and Perkins, 1838), 92–93.

KARL BARTH. Karl Barth, *Fifty Prayers*, translated from the German by David Carl Stassen (Louisville: Westminster John Knox, 2008), 11–12. Used with permission.

JOSEPH BAYLY. Adapted, with permission, from "A Psalm of Single-Mindedness" by Joseph Bayly, in *Psalms of My Life* (Elgin, IL: Life Journey Books, 1987 [orig. Wheaton: Tyndale House, 1969]), 10–11.

BEDE THE VENERABLE. Attributed to Bede. A memorial inscription above Bede's tomb in the Galilee Chapel in Durham Cathedral contains a similar affirmation, from Bede's commentary on Revelation 2:28: "Christ is the Morning Star who when the night of this world is past brings to his saints the promise of the light of life and opens everlasting day."

BENEDICT OF NURSIA. This prayer is commonly attributed to St. Benedict, though its origins are uncertain. Found in the "Prayers During the Day" section of *Common Worship: Daily Prayer* (London: Church House, 2005), produced by the Church of England. https://www.churchofengland.org /prayer-and-worship/worship-texts-and-resources/common-worship/daily -prayer/prayer-during-day.

DIETRICH BONHOEFFER. "Prayer in Particular Need" (Letter #78), Tegel, November 1943, in *Letters and Papers from Prison*, Dietrich Bonhoeffer Works, vol. 8, ed. John W. de Gruchy (Minneapolis: Fortress, 2010), 198. This English translation from the German is by Isabel Best. Used with permission.

WILLIAM BOOTH. This prayer by William Booth first appeared in the April 14, 1894, issue of the Salvation Army magazine *The War Cry*. It was later reworked into a hymn.

JOHN BRADFORD. From "A Prayer for Deliverance from Sin, and to Be Restored to God's Grace and Favour Again," in *Writings of the Rev. John Bradford* (London: Religious Tract Society, 1827), 429–30.

DAVID BRAINERD. From a diary entry dated April 4, 1742, in *The Diary of David Brainerd*, vol. 1 (London: Andrew Melrose, 1902), 35–36.

ANNE BRONTË. The final two stanzas of the poem "Confidence," which Anne's sister Charlotte published posthumously in a volume with *Wuthering Heights*, *Agnes Grey*, and a selection of other "literary remains" by Anne and Emily (London: Smith, Elder, 1851), 494.

MARTIN BUCER. This prayer for illumination preceding the public reading of Scripture in worship is from Martin Bucer's Strasbourg Liturgy of 1539.

See *Liturgies of the Western Church*, selected, translated, and introduced by Bard Thompson (Minneapolis: Augsburg Fortress, 1961), 170.

JOHN CALVIN. Adapted by Timothy Keller from John Calvin's "Prayer for the Morning," in *Calvin's Tracts, containing Treatises on the Sacraments, Catechism of the Church of Geneva, Forms of Prayer, and Confessions of Faith*, vol. 2, translated from the original Latin and French by Henry Beveridge (Edinburgh: Calvin Translation Society, 1849), 95–96.

AMY CARMICHAEL. "For Our Children," in Amy Carmichael, *Toward Jerusalem: Poems of Faith* (London: SPCK, 1987), 106. Italics original.

THOMAS THEULLOSSON CARTER. An uncredited Advent prayer from "Devotions for the Church's Seasons" in T. T. Carter, ed., *The Treasury of Devotion: A Manual of Prayer for General and Daily Use* (London: Rivingtons, 1875), 151.

CATHERINE OF SIENA. Excerpts from *Catherine of Siena: The Dialogue*, The Classics of Western Spirituality, translated from the Italian by Suzanne Noffke, OP (Mahwah, NJ: Paulist Press, 1980), 364–65. Copyright © 1980 Paulist Press, Inc. Used by permission of Paulist Press, www.paulistpress.com.

THOMAS CHISHOLM. "Great Is Thy Faithfulness" first appeared in *Songs of Salvation and Service*, ed. William M. Runyan (Chicago: Hope Publishing, 1923).

TITUS COAN. From a letter to his future wife, Fidelia Church, quoted in Lydia Bingham Coan, *Titus Coan: A Memorial* (Chicago: Fleming H. Revell, 1884), 5.

JOHN COSIN. John Cosin, *A Collection of Private Devotions for the Hours of Prayer* (Oxford: James Parker, 1867), 77.

THOMAS CRANMER. From "Daily Evening Prayer: Rite One," in the Book of Common Prayer, www.bcponline.org/DailyOffice/ep1.html.

DIONYSIUS OF TEL MAHRE. Lightly edited from J. Manning Potts, ed., *Prayers of the Middle Ages* (Nashville: Upper Room, 1908).

THOMAS DORSEY. "Precious Lord, Take My Hand," words and music by Thomas A. Dorsey. © 1938 (renewed) Warner-Tamerlane Publishing Corp. All rights reserved. Used by permission of Alfred Music.

CHARLOTTE ELLIOTT. "Just as I Am" was first published in the second edition of *The Invalid's Hymn Book*, ed. Charlotte Elliott (Dublin: John Robertson, 1841).

EPHREM THE SYRIAN. The so-called "Lenten Prayer of St. Ephrem" is not found in the Syriac corpus of Ephrem's writings. While it does not come from his hand, Orthodox scholars regard it as part of his "received legacy" handed down through subsequent monastic communities, and it has long been used in Byzantine Rite liturgies during Great Lent. See the paper by the Rt. Revd. Prof. Irenei, Bishop of Sacramento, "The Lenten Prayer—'of St. Ephrem'? A Few Observations in a Varied Textual Tradition," delivered at the Fourth International Patristics Conference of the Postgraduate Institute of Saints Athanasius and Methodius in Moscow in April 2017, https://www.wadiocese.org/files/General-2017/Bishop-Irenei-St-Ephraim-Moscow/4en bpireneiprayerofstephraim.pdf.

EUSEBIUS OF CAESAREA. In the fifth century, Joannes Stobaeus compiled an anthology of extracts from Greek authors in his *Florilegium*, including this prayer, which he ascribes to Eusebius. This English translation by Gilbert Murray is from Gilbert Murray, *Five Stages of Greek Religion* (New York: Columbia University Press, 1925), 236–37, whose direct source was F. W. A. (Friedrich Wilhelm August) Mullach, *Fragmenta philosophorum graecorum*, vol. 3 (Paris, 1879), 7.

FRANÇOIS FÉNELON. Lightly edited from "A Prayer of Fénelon," in *Selections from the World's Devotional Classics*, vol. 1, *Tobit to Chrysostom*, ed. Robert Scott and George W. Gilmore (New York: Funk & Wagnalls, 1916), 207. See also François Fénelon, *Meditations on the Heart of God*, Christian Classics, trans. Robert J. Edmonson (Brewster, MA: Paraclete, 1997).

JOHN FLAVEL. Lightly edited from "Of the Solemn Consecration of the Mediator" in John Flavel, *The Fountain of Life Opened Up; or, a Display of Christ in His Essential and Mediatorial Glory, Containing Forty-Two Sermons* (London, 1671).

FRANCIS OF ASSISI. This prayer was originally published anonymously in French in 1912 by the Catholic association La Ligue de la Sainte-Messe (The Holy Mass League) in their magazine *La Clochette* (The Little Bell) under the title "Belle prière à faire pendant la messe" (A Beautiful Prayer to Say During the Mass). The first known translation in English appeared in the book *Living Courageously* by Kirby Page (New York: Farrar & Rinehart, 1936), where it is attributed to St. Francis.

FURSEY OF IRELAND. "Lorica of St. Fursa," in *Prayers from the Ancient Celtic Church*, collected, translated, and edited by Paul C. Stratman (self-pub., 2018), 6. Used with permission. The only known copy of Fursey's lorica survives in a Middle Irish collection of theological works composed in the fifteenth and sixteenth centuries, known as the *Leabhar Uí Maolconaire* (British Library, Add MS 30512).

GREGORY OF NYSSA. From "On the Baptism of Christ: A Sermon for the Day of Lights," translated from the Greek by Walter Mitchell in *Early Christian Prayers*, ed. Adalbert Hamman, OFM (Chicago: Henry Regnery, 1961), 169–70.

JANE GREY. *The Lady Jane Grey's Prayer Book: British Library Harley Manuscript 2342, Fully Illustrated and Transcribed*, introduced by J. Stephan Edwards (Palm Springs, CA: Old John, 2016).

GUIGO II. *The Ladder of Monks: A Letter on the Contemplative Life, and Twelve Meditations*, translated from the Latin by Edmund Colledge, OSA, and James Walsh, SJ (New York: Image / Doubleday, 1978), 73.

HENRY GUINNESS. From "Sermon 13: The Woman of Samaria," in Rev. H. Grattan Guinness, *Sermons* (London: James Nisbet, 1860), 304.

GEORGE HERBERT. Lightly edited from George Herbert, *A Priest to the Temple; or, The Country Parson, His Character, and Rule of Holy Life* (1652), in *The Works of George Herbert in Prose and Verse* (New York: John Wurtele Lovell, 1881), 401.

HILDEGARD OF BINGEN. Adapted from the writings of Hildegard, in Robert Van de Weyer, ed., *The HarperCollins Book of Prayers: A Treasury of Prayers through the Ages* (Edison, NJ: Castle Books, 1997 [orig. 1993]), 196–97. I couldn't locate the original source material for the first stanza, but the other two stanzas appear to be based on two of the antiphons in Hildegard's *Symphonia*: "Spiritus sanctus vivificans" (Holy Spirit, Living and Life-Giving) and "O eterne Deus" (O Eternal God).

IRENAEUS OF LYONS. Adapted from J. Manning Potts, ed., *Prayers of the Early Church* (Nashville: Upper Room, 1908), which attributes the prayer to Irenaeus and cites the Old Gallican Sacramentary as its source.

JULIAN OF NORWICH. *Revelations of Divine Love*, chap. 5. Translated into modern English.

MACRINA THE YOUNGER. Gregory of Nyssa recorded this prayer of his sister's as she lay dying. Lightly edited from St. Gregory of Nyssa, *The Life of St. Macrina*, translated from the Greek by W. K. Lowther Clarke (London: Society for Promoting Christian Knowledge, 1916), 55–57.

HELEN KELLER. Helen Keller delivered her "Prayer for Peace" Sunday, April 5, 1936, at the "East of Suez" bazaar hosted by the New History Society, and it was published the following month in *New History* 5, no. 8 (May 1936): 1. Accessed from the Hellen Keller Archive, American Foundation for the Blind, https://www.afb.org/HelenKellerArchive?a=d&d=A-HK02-B213-F02-005.

JOHANNES KEPLER. From *Harmonices Mundi* (Harmonies of the World) (1619), bk. 5, chap. 9. Paraphrased by Matt Thiele, https://www.justprayer .gracespace.info/astronomers-prayer-johannes-kepler/, from a public-domain translation of the Latin by Charles Glenn Wallis, https://sacred -texts.com/astro/how/how10.htm. Used with permission.

LUCY LARCOM. "Our Prayers," from Lucy Larcom, *At the Beautiful Gate, and Other Songs of Faith* (Boston: Houghton Mifflin, 1892), 40–41.

ROBERT LAWSON. "Prayer for Freedom from Race Prejudice," in *The Anthropology of Jesus Christ Our Kinsman* (1925); quoted in James Washington, ed., *Conversations with God: Two Centuries of Prayers by African Americans* (New York: HarperCollins, 1994), 143.

MADELEINE L'ENGLE. Excerpts from the poem "Lines Scribbled on an Envelope While Riding the 104 Broadway Bus" by Madeleine L'Engle, from *Lines Scribbled on an Envelope, and Other Poems* (New York: Farrar, Straus and Giroux, 1969). Published in *The Ordering of Love: The New and Collected Poems of Madeleine L'Engle* (Colorado Springs: Shaw / WaterBrook, 2005), 7–8. Used by permission of the Estate of Madeleine L'Engle.

WILHELM LOEHE. Lightly edited from the "Morning Prayer" in the "Breviary for the Use of the Pastor," in Wilhelm Loehe, *Liturgy for Christian Congregations of the Lutheran Faith*, translated from the German by the Rev. F. C. Longaker (Newport, KY: n.p., 1902), 6.

MARTIN LUTHER. This prayer is from Luther's Sommerpostille (Summer Postil), a collection of his sermonic writings covering Easter through Ordinary Time, first published in 1526. The English translation is in the public domain.

GEORGE MACDONALD. "January 10," from George MacDonald, *A Book of Strife in the Form of the Diary of an Old Soul* (privately printed, 1880; London: Longmans, Green, 1885).

HENRY EDWARD MANNING. Lightly edited from Henry Edward, Archbishop of Westminster, *The Internal Mission of the Holy Ghost* (London: Burns and Oates, 1875), 29.

GEORGE MATHESON. George Matheson, *Searchings in the Silence: A Series of Devotional Meditations*, 2nd ed. (London: Cassell, 1895), 59–60.

F. B. MEYER. From "The Lesson of the Thorn-Bush" (February 23), on Exodus 3:2–4, in F. B. Meyer, *Our Daily Walk: Daily Readings* (Ross-shire, Scotland: Christian Focus, 2015).

JOHN MILTON. Adapted from *Paradise Lost*, bk. 1, lines 17–26.

THOMAS MORE. According to the Center for Thomas More Studies, this was Thomas's last prayer, written while he was imprisoned in the Tower of London awaiting his execution. Adapted from *The Wisdom and Wit of Blessed Thomas More: Being Extracts from Such of His Works as Were Written in English* (New York: Catholic Publication Society, 1892), 94–97. The critical edition of this prayer is in volume 13 of *The Complete Works of St. Thomas More* (New Haven: Yale University Press, 1976), 228–31.

MOTHER TERESA. Susan Conroy, who spent a summer working with Mother Teresa, quotes this prayer that she prayed in her book *Mother Teresa's Lessons of Love and Secrets of Sanctity* (Huntington, IN: Our Sunday Visitor, 2003). The first three sentences of the prayer appear to have originated with Mother Teresa, but the rest is taken from this prayer by John Henry Newman: "Stay with me, and then I shall begin to shine as Thou shinest: so to shine as to be a light to others. The light, O Jesus, will be all from Thee. None of it will be mine. No merit to me. It will be Thou who shinest through me upon others. O let me thus praise Thee, in the way Thou dost love best, by shining on all those around me. Give light to them as well as to me; light them with me, through me. Teach me to show Thy praise, Thy truth, Thy will. Make me preach Thee without preaching—not by words, but by my example and by the catching force, the sympathetic influence, of what I do—by my visible resemblance to Thy saints, and the evident fullness of the love which my heart bears to Thee." *Meditations and Devotions of the Late Cardinal Newman*, 3rd ed. (London: Longmans, Green, 1894), 500–501.

MALCOLM MUGGERIDGE. Malcolm Muggeridge, *Conversion: The Spiritual Journey of a Twentieth-Century Pilgrim* (Eugene, OR: Wipf & Stock, 2005 [orig. 1988]), 75. Used by permission of Wipf and Stock Publishers, www.wipfandstock.com.

ANDREW MURRAY. Lightly edited from the Rev. Andrew Murray, *With Christ in the School of Prayer: Thoughts on Our Training for the Ministry of Intercession* (New York: Fleming H. Revell, 1895), 38.

WATCHMAN NEE. Hymn No. 185 in *The Collected Works of Watchman Nee*, vol. 23, *The Song of Songs and Hymns* (n.p.: Living Stream Ministry, 1993). Set to music in 1976 by Sister Mimi Lam.

JOHN HENRY NEWMAN. Adapted from the conclusion to Sermon 20, "Wisdom and Innocence," in John Henry Newman, *Sermons Bearing on Subjects of the Day* (London: Rivingtons, 1843), 347.

REINHOLD NIEBUHR. This prayer exists in many forms, and its original authorship is disputed, but it is most strongly connected with Reinhold Niebuhr, who, when interviewed for a January 1950 *Grapevine* article, said, "Of course, it may have been spooking around for years, even centuries, but I don't think so. I honestly do believe that I wrote it myself." It first publicly appeared with Niebuhr's name attached to it in *A Book of Prayers and Services for the Armed Forces* (1944), compiled by the Federal Council of Churches of Christ in America, but Fred R. Shapiro has found a recorded version, attributed to "R. N.," appearing as early as October 31, 1932, in a diary entry by Winnifred Crane Wygal, an early disseminator of the prayer who had studied under Niebuhr at Union and worked for the YWCA. The version reproduced in *Prayers from the Cloud* is, according to Niebuhr's daughter, Elisabeth Sifton, the one preferred by Niebuhr. See Elisabeth Sifton, *Serenity Prayer: Faith and Politics in Times of Peace and War* (New York: Norton, 2003), and Fred Shapiro, "How I Discovered I Was Wrong about the Origin of the Serenity Prayer," Religion News Service, May 15, 2014, https://religionnews .com/2014/05/15/commentary-discovered-wrong-origin-serenity-prayer/.

HENRI NOUWEN. Henri J. M. Nouwen, *A Cry for Mercy: Prayers from the Genesee* (New York: Image / Doubleday, 2002), 30–31. Copyright © 1981 Henri J. M. Nouwen. Used by permission of Doubleday, an imprint of the Knopf Doubleday Publishing Group, a division of Penguin Random House LLC. All rights reserved.

PHOEBE PALMER. Excerpts from "A Covenant," in Phoebe Palmer, *Present to My Christian Friend on Entire Devotion to God*, 14th ed. (London: Alexander Heylin, 1860), 96–100.

BLAISE PASCAL. Lightly edited from *The Thoughts of Blaise Pascal* [*Pensées*], translated from the French by C. Kegan Paul (London: George Bell and Sons, 1905), 234.

ALAN PATON. Alan Paton, *Instrument of Thy Peace* (New York: Seabury, 1968), 13–14. Used by permission of the Alan Paton Will Trust.

PATRICK OF IRELAND. "St. Patrick's Breastplate," translated from the Irish by Noel Dermot O'Donoghue in James P. Mackey, ed., *An Introduction to Celtic Christianity* (London: T&T Clark, 1989), 45–64.

WILLIAM PENN. *The Oxford Book of Prayer* #541 attributes this prayer to William Penn, as do numerous other anthologies, but no original source is given. It was popularized by Fr. Bede Jarrett, OP (1881–1934), who credited Penn, and adapted by Rossiter W. Raymond (1840–1918) in his poem "Death Is Only an Horizon."

POLYCARP. From the *Martyrium Polycarpi* (Martyrdom of Polycarp), chap. 14, an anonymous account written after Polycarp's death, translated from the Greek by J. B. Lightfoot in *The Apostolic Fathers*, vol. 1, part 2: *S. Ignatius, S. Polycarp* (London: Macmillan, 1885). Modernized by Stephen Tomkins for "Module 103: Polycarp's Martyrdom," Christian History Institute, https://christianhistoryinstitute.org/study/module/polycarp.

RICHARD OF CHICHESTER. J. Manning Potts, ed., *Prayers of the Middle Ages* (Nashville: Upper Room, 1908).

ROBERT ROBINSON. The hymn first appeared in *A Collection of Hymns for the Use of the Church of Christ: Meeting in Angel-Alley* (London, 1759).

CHRISTINA ROSSETTI. Adapted from Christina G. Rossetti, *Annus Domini: A Prayer for Each Day of the Year Founded on a Text of Holy Scripture* (Oxford: James Parker, 1874), no. 165.

GIROLAMO SAVONAROLA. Lightly edited from Charles Leffingwell, ed., *A Book of Prayers: Together with Psalms and Hymns and Spiritual Songs, Ancient and Modern* (Milwaukee: Morehouse, 1921), 44. For the original Latin text and its translation in full, see Girolamo Savonarola, OP, *Prison Meditations on Psalms 51 and 31*, Reformation Texts with Translation (1350–1650), vol. 1, introduced, translated, and edited by John Patrick Donnelly, SJ (Milwaukee: Marquette University Press, 1991).

DOROTHY SAYERS. "Hymn in Contemplation of Sudden Death," in Dorothy L. Sayers, *Op. I.* (Oxford: B. H. Blackwell, 1916).

IDA SCUDDER. The medical school that Ida Scudder founded, CMC Vellore, quotes "Aunt Ida's Prayer" at https://www.cmch-vellore.edu/SinglePage.aspx?pid=P171127016&mid=M171211128.

FULTON SHEEN. Fulton Sheen, *Your Life Is Worth Living: 50 Lessons to Deepen Your Faith* (New York: Image, 2019), 402.

CHARLES SPURGEON. Charles Haddon Spurgeon, *Illustrations and Meditations: Or, Flowers from a Puritan's Garden, Distilled and Dispensed* (New York: Funk & Wagnalls, 1883), 18.

SOJOURNER TRUTH. *The Narrative of Sojourner Truth*, dictated by Sojourner Truth and edited by Olive Gilbert (Boston, 1850), 70.

C. T. STUDD. C. T. Studd, *The Chocolate Soldier: Or, Heroism—The Lost Chord of Christianity* (Fort Washington, PA: Christian Literature Crusade, n.d. [1912]).

HARRIET BEECHER STOWE. No. 676 in Henry Ward Beecher, ed., *Plymouth Collection of Hymns: For the Use of Christian Congregations* (New York: A. S. Barnes, 1855). This is one of three hymns by Harriet that appears in this hymnal, which was edited by her brother.

JEREMY TAYLOR. Adapted from "Another Form of Prayer for the Morning," sec. 4, in Jeremy Taylor, *The Rule and Exercises of Holy Living* (London, 1650).

TERESA OF ÁVILA. *The Book of My Life*, translated from the Spanish by Mirabai Starr (Boston: New Seeds, 2007), 7, 12. Copyright © 2007 Mirabai Starr. Reprinted by arrangement with The Permissions Company, LLC, on behalf of New Seeds Books, an imprint of Shambhala Publications Inc., Boulder, Colorado, www.shambhala.com.

GERHARD TERSTEEGEN. Mary Wilder Tileston, ed., *Prayers Ancient and Modern* (New York: Doubleday, 1897), 100.

THEODORE THE STUDITE. Lightly edited from J. Manning Potts, ed., *Prayers of the Middle Ages* (Nashville: Upper Room, 1908). The third part of this composite prayer comes from a letter Theodore wrote around 809–811 to the nun Anna, instructing her how to pray. See an English translation of the letter by Archimandrite Ephrem Lash at https://web.archive.org/web/2007 0213231706/http://web.ukonline.co.uk/ephrem/Anna-ep.htm.

THÉRÈSE OF LISIEUX. Excerpts from "My Song of Today" (original title: "Mon Chant d'Aujourd'hui"), in *The Poetry of Saint Thérèse of Lisieux*, translated from the French by Donald Kinney, OCD (Washington, DC: ICS Publications, 1995), 51–53. Used by permission of the publisher.

THOMAS À KEMPIS. *The Imitation of Christ by Thomas à Kempis: A New Reading of the 1441 Latin Autograph Manuscript* by William C. Creasy, 2nd ed. (Macon, GA: Mercer University Press, 2007), 72. Used by permission of Mercer University Press.

THOMAS AQUINAS. Lightly edited from J. Manning Potts, ed., *Prayers of the Middle Ages* (Nashville: Upper Room, 1908). Originally written in Latin, this prayer is excerpted from a longer prayer by Aquinas titled "Ad vitam sapienter instituendam" (For Ordering a Life Wisely), which begins, "Concede mihi, misericors Deus . . ."

TIKHON OF ZADONSK. St. Tychon, "Confession and Thanksgiving to Christ," in G. P. Fedotov, ed., *A Treasury of Russian Spirituality* (New York: Sheed & Ward, 1948).

EVELYN UNDERHILL. Lightly edited from Evelyn Underhill, *The Mount of Purification: With Meditations and Prayers, 1949, and Collected Papers, 1946* (London: Longmans Green, 1960), 126–27.

ANNA WARING. Anna Letitia Waring, *Hymns and Meditations*, 4th ed. (London, 1854), 78–83. The first line originally read, "Go not far from me, O my strength," but editor James Martineau changed its last word to "God" in his compilation *Hymns of Praise and Prayer* (London, 1873), and this change has stuck.

ANNA WARNER. The first and last stanzas of "For Victory," in Anna Warner, *Hymns of the Church Militant* (New York: Robert Carter & Brothers, 1858), 161–63.

ISAAC WATTS. Originally published in Isaac Watts, *The Psalms of David, Imitated in the Language of the New Testament* (London, 1719).

JOHN WESLEY. "John Wesley's Covenant Prayer," in *The United Methodist Book of Worship* (Nashville: United Methodist Publishing House, 1992).

SUSANNA WESLEY. *The Prayers of Susanna Wesley*, ed. W. L. Doughty, Clarion Classics (Grand Rapids: Zondervan, 1984), 25.

ULRICH ZWINGLI. *The Worship Sourcebook*, 2nd ed. (Grand Rapids: Calvin Institute of Christian Worship, Faith Alive Christian Resources, and Baker Books, 2013), 142.

Index of Authors